I0015219

Python programming crash course

This book includes

Python for beginners

Python for data science

Computer programming for beginners

Tony f. charles

Python for beginners

Introduction

Python is a great language to start your programming journey. It has an easy syntax that makes sense to non-programming professionals. In the background, it's based on the C language which makes it extremely powerful. Since created by Van Rossum in 1991, Python has remained an open source project. It is for this reason you will find a lot of online tutorials and resources about Python.

Today, more fields than ever before are replying on computers to achieve results. Whether you are an aspiring social worker or a game designer, you require a particular degree of computer knowledge to get employment. Even if it's not a requirement, you can increase your productivity by automating your daily tasks. Consider you are a social worker who has to send regular email updates to your boss about the cases you work everyday. Since you already record notes on your computer, you might be able to write a script to extract information from your notes and send emails to your boss automatically at the end of your day. This is just one example, and I am sure you can think about a dozen similar tasks that you do that can be automated.

If you are starting with programming and have no knowledge about computers and programming, this book is written for you. You will find initial chapters easier to understand and as you progress to later chapters, you will have better skills and we will cover more advanced topics. This book is written in one flow and it's better to not skip any topic, let alone an entire chapter.

The software industry is changing rapidly and by the time you are finished with this book, there might be better techniques or tools available. This book focuses on using multiple tools to get the same results so the following can be instilled in your mind: "It doesn't matter what tools you use, the only thing that makes headlines is the end-product." I have high hopes this book will make your programming journey easier.

Chapter 1: Computer Science and Mathematics

Computers were developed by scientists to solve problems. Mathematics is the scientific language to solve problems. Therefore, computers and mathematics are inseparable. Computers utilize mathematical concepts to identify and solve problems. They are much better in sequential processing and more recently in multitasking different processes. Take the example of a french fries seller. He peels and cuts 50 potatoes all by himself. With time, more people start to buy fries from him and he needs to peel and cut more potatoes. He can hire helpers who he will have to pay per hour and also afford their medical and accommodate for their availability. The other option is to get a computer aided automated machine that takes the potatoes, washes, peels and then cuts them according to given criteria. The initial setup cost might be high but due to low operational cost, this is the better option. Not only the cost, the machine will be able to process more potatoes much quicker compared to human helpers.

This is how computers are changing everyone's lives. The cellphone you use all the time is also a computer, a small yet very sophisticated and powerful computer. Let's look at the history of computers.

History of Computers

In the 1880 US census, the population was determined to be a little over 50 million, 50,189,209 to be exact. It took 7 years for the US government to compile the census results and come up with the total number. There was definitely a need to process the census data faster. This need resulted in the invention of punch card computers that were gigantic machines. But, the concept of computers even predates this era.

Abacus

Not a computer but a counting tool, Abacus has been used for centuries by many ancient civilizations to count. How the tool came into existence is a complete mystery. It is still used today to teach children and visually impaired persons how to count.

Abacus is based upon the concept of coding - representing values with symbols. In the case of abacus, numbers are represented by beads and their values are determined by their positions.

1801: To automate the weaving process of different fabric designs, Joseph Marie Jacquard invented a punch card reading loom. This punch card reading technology was later used by electronic computers in the early 20th century.

1822: People have hated memorizing multiplication tables for ages. Want proof? Charles Babbage, an English mathematician, invented a steam-powered machine to calculate the number tables. The English government funded project ultimately failed, but laid the foundation for computers developed later on.

1890: Remember when we said it took US government seven years to process the 1880 census? In the 1890 census, Herman Hollerith solved the issue by designing a system based on punch cards. It saved $5 million for the government and completed the process in only three years. The company Herman founded later became IBM.

1936: The modern computer is a good example of a Turing machine, a concept coined by Alan Turing in 1936 about a machine that can compute anything that's possible to compute.

1937: Up till this year, computers were electro-mechanical machines. A physics and mathematics professor at Iowa State, J.V. Atanasoff, attempted to build a computer without moving mechanical parts. Did he succeed? Time to do some Googling!

1939: The now globally recognized tech-giant, manufacturers of computer systems and peripherals, the "hp" company was founded by Bill Hewlett and David Packard in a garage of the city of Palo Alto, California.

1941: With the help of his graduate student Clifford Berry, J.V. Atanasoff one ups his previous achievement by designing a computer that could simultaneously solve 29 equations. The computer was the first of its kind because it could hold information in its memory.

1943-44: Two University of Pennsylvania professors, J.P. Eckert and John Mauchly, invent the Electronic Numerical Integrator and Calculator (ENIAC). A precursor to digital computers, it was physically enormous comprising of more than 17,500 vacuum tubes in a 20ft by 40ft assembly.

1946: The United States Census Bureau funded a contract for Mauchly and Eckert to build Universal Automatic Computer (UNIVAC). UNIVAC became the first commercially available computer and was widely used by government departments and research, financial and aviation institutions.

1947: The era of electronic computers started with the invention of the solid state transistor by William Shockley, Walter Brattain and John Bardeen of Bell laboratories. The transistor worked as a virtual switch that could either be off or on to store information. It was much smaller in size, consumed much less power and generated much less heat compared to vacuum tubes.

1953: COmmon Business-Oriented Language (COBOL), the first programming language, was invented by Grace Hooper. Thomas Watson Jr. invents the IBM 701 EDPM for the sole purpose of enabling the United Nations to monitor the Korean region during the Korean War.

1954: With computers becoming more commonly used by various companies, the need for a better programming language became apparent. A team of IBM programmers headed by John Backus developed a programming language named FORMula TRANslation (FORTRAN).

1958: Thanks to rapid advancements in the field of electronics, Jack Kilby and Robert Noyce developed the first integrated circuit to be used as a computer chip. The Nobel Prize in the field of Physics was awarded to Kilby in 2000, more than 40 years after his incredible feat.

1964: A computer with a mouse and Graphical User Interface (GUI) is demonstrated by Douglas Engelbert as a modern computer prototype. The purpose was to introduce a highly accessible computer model that the general public could feel comfortable with. Computers were no longer just a scientist's play toy.

1962: There was no compatibility and standardization as different manufacturers independently designed computer systems. The issue was addressed by a team of Bell Labs programmers who created UNIX, a C language based operating system. The operating system could be run on various computer systems of that time. The era of system independent software was kickstarted even though UNIX was mostly deployed on mainframe systems by corporations instead of personal computers due to slow performance.

1970: Intel joined the computer race by launching the first temporary memory chips known as Intel 1103 Dynamic Random Access Memory (DRAM).

1973: Connecting multiple computers and/or hardware to combine computational power became easy when one of the research staff members at Xerox, Robert Metcalfe, invented the Ethernet protocol.

1974-77: Personal computers became more popular which led to the unveiling of several different models in the market including IBM 5100, Scelbi & Mark-8 Altair and the Radio Shack's "Trash 80", model TRS-80. Another popular personal computer from that era is the Commodore PET.

1975: The Altair 8080 got featured in the Popular Electronics (PE) magazine as the first true minicomputer for personal use that provide the same computational power of commercial computers. It inspires two computer enthusiasts Paul Allen and Bill Gates to write software for the popular minicomputer. Both later start a software firm on the back of this successful endeavour, called Microsoft.

1976: Apple Computers went operational led by the Two Steves, Steve Jobs and Steve Wozniak. Their first computer Apple 1 was launched on April Fool's day and was the first computer that used a single circuit board.

1977: The Trash 80 demand rose so high among the general public that Radio Shack had to manufacture more than the initial 3,000 unit production. The multipurpose nature of the computer made it hugely popular. In the same year, the Two Steves incorporated Apple and launched the Apple II during the West Coast Computer Fair. The computer offered color graphics and better storage via a drive for audio cassettes.

1978: The first spreadsheet software, called VisiCalc, got introduced. No one knows that name today!

1979: The first word processing software WordStar was launched by MicroPro International headed by Rob Barnaby. The software had various editing and formatting options including the ability to add margins, word wrap and print documents. The company went with a modernistic approach with the software and did not include a command mode which was usually a feature in software of that era. Another great software of that era that did not make it through the years.

1981: The first personal computer made of IBM's Intel hardware and Microsoft's MS DOS operating system, named "Acorn" was launched. Even today, the majority of personal computers have the combination of IBM and Microsoft products. Acorn offered two floppy disk drives and supported a color monitor. For the first time, the computer was sold through third party distributors and was popularly referred to as the PC.

1983: Apple introduced the first personal computer with a true GUI, named Lisa. The computer interface featured graphical icons and dropdown menus. The product flopped but paved the way for the future Apple computer system line of Macintosh. The same year, Gavilan Computer Corp. unveiled the Gavilan SC, the first widely recognized portable personal computer (laptop).

1985: To counter Apple's Lida, Microsoft introduced Windows which became the most widely used operating system in personal computers. In the same year, Commodore launched the Amiga 1000 that had enhanced audio and video abilities. In the same year, a Massachusetts based computer manufacturer Symbolics, purchased the first dot com website domain in the world: "symbolics.com". At this time, there wasn't even a concept of Internet history.

1986: Compaq launched the Deskpro 386 that had a 32bit architecture offering better performance than the competition to the extent it rivalled the mainframes of that era.

1990: In any organization of this era there were several hundred computers, and there was also a protocol to connect them (ethernet), but there was no good way to present information. A European Organization for Nuclear Research (commonly known as CERN, which is short for the french "Conseil européen pour la recherche nucléaire") researcher, Tim Berners-Lee, developed the HyperText Markup Language (HTML) which later became the language of the World Wide Web.

1993: Intel introduced the revolutionary Pentium processors that enabled high quality graphics and audio services to be offered in personal computers.

1994: The launch of hit video games including "Descent", "Alone in the Dark 2", "Magic Carpet", "Command & Conquer", "Little Big Adventure" and "Theme Park" meant the computers were not just for work, people were actively using them for entertainment. There was a demand for better performing computers.

1996: The search engine most people use today, Google, went live developed by Larry Page and Sergey Brin.

1997: Apple was struggling and in a legal dispute with Microsoft with the allegation that Microsoft copied the design and feel of its operating system. Apple took back the case after Microsoft invested an amount of $150 million in Apple.

1999: More mobility freedom became possible for the personal computer users after WiFi was introduced which meant internet and local connections could be made without the need for physical wires.

2001: The rivalry between Apple and Microsoft intensified after Apple released the newly designed Mac OS X. It was an instant hit as it offered secured memory architecture, as well as superior and faster multitasking by preserving software states. As a response, Microsoft released the Windows XP with a distinct GUI and advanced features.

2003: Albeit having a much smaller market share, AMD one ups Intel this time by launching the first ever 64bit system known as Athlon 64 which became an instant hit.

2004: Mozilla launches Firefox browser to rival the widely used Internet Explorer by

Microsoft. Although not very intuitive, Internet Explorer was widely used because it was bundled with the popular Windows operating system. Mark Zuckerberg launched Facebook which was a social media platform.

2005: YouTube, the biggest video sharing platform today, was designed and launched by three PayPal employees, Jawed Karim, Steve Chen and Chad Hurley. Google acquired the Linux-based operating system for mobile devices known as Android.

2006: Apple designed the first mobile computer (laptop) MacBook Pro and the desktop computer iMac both of which used an Intel-based dual core system. Nintendo Wii gaming console became available in the market that had games based on motion and gesture detection.

2007: Apple released the groundbreaking smartphone with the brand name iPhone which remained the best-selling cell phone for a long time.

2009: Windows 7 was launched by Microsoft which became widely popular and had advanced capabilities including touch and speech recognition.

2010: Apple reignited consumer interest in tablets by launching the iPad.

2011: Google released the Chrome OS based laptop with the brand name Chromebook.

2012: Facebook gained 1 billion users, becoming the most significant social media platform.

2015: Apple released another technically advanced device: the Apple Watch. Microsoft released the final version of Windows, Windows 10, but still kept support for Windows 7 for years due to its wide use.

2016: Not the first quantum computer, but the first reprogrammable quantum computer was created. Before this, quantum computers were manufactured for specific purposes.

2017: Big improvements were made in the field of "molecular informatics", the science of creating computers using molecules as processing units.

The advancements in computer systems grow everyday. The silicon based electronics have almost reached their limits. There are various researches going on to find a better base for electronic devices, but they are still far from commercial use.

Computer Architecture

The science of joining computer hardware and software to create unique computational systems is called computer architecture. It has evolved many times during the years as the applications of computers changed. Von Neumann architecture is the most famous computer architecture that relates to modern digital computers. According to this architecture, all computer systems are more or less comprised of following main parts.

Central Processing Unit (CPU)

The brain of a computer, the central processing unit, processes the given input and generates the desired output. The CPU itself is comprised of various parts.

Control Unit

Control Unit controls all the aspects of the CPU so the latter can process data according to set instructions. The supported set of instructions are stored in the permanent memory (Read Only Memory - ROM). It also controls the flow of data within the computer and provides signals for timing operations. If you are a gamer or a professional who has to deal with high quality graphics, you might have tweaked the clock speed of your computer's graphics unit. This is direct interaction with the computer's control unit.

Processor

The processor performs the actual computations. It houses the logic circuits and onboard caches, known as registers, for fast temporary data storage. Registers, which should not be confused with the main memory (RAM), enable the processor to store intermediate data generated during complex computations. The logic circuitry has electronic gates that operate on given data in different ways as told by the given instructions.

Main Memory

The Random Access Memory (RAM) is referred to as the main memory of a computer. Why? Because all the currently running applications are kept here until something is no longer needed. Modern computers have very large RAMs which enables them to hold many dormant applications for a longer time which makes multitasking and application boot up time very fast. Failure of power usually erases the contents of the RAM.

Input Systems

There are various input peripherals that have been developed for different purposes. The most common is the keyboard and the mouse. We have now touch screens, touch pads, voice (microphones) and image recognition (cameras) built into the computer. You can also use a scanner to scan hardcopy documents for easy processing and transmission.

Output Systems

Just like input devices, there are several output peripherals, the most common being the monitor and speaker. The other commonly known output device is the printer. It's interesting to note that the output devices are very few as compared to the input devices. It shows that the focus of computer architecture has always been to enable computers to take input so they can process it in the desired way.

More Components in A Modern Computer

A modern computer has a lot of different components added for enhanced processing capabilities.

External Memory

If you look at the computer architecture, you would notice there's no storage available for the user to store any information. The ROM is read only and houses the instructions and the RAM is temporary. In earlier computers, there were floppy disk drives that acted as an external memory so the computer user could save any information. In later computers, a hard disk was introduced as a permanent part of the computer system that was used to store all the information. With the advancement in memory storage, more devices were introduced such as CDs, DVDs and now the most common, USB flash drives.

Graphics Processing Unit (GPU)

Modern computers are frequently used in applications that demand high quality graphics. Video games have become very common, professionals have to deal with creation and editing of high quality graphics. Even watching high definition movies takes a lot of processing power. To remove excessive load from the CPU of a computer, a standalone processing unit is added to handle all graphics related tasks. Not only does it divide the load, it also divides the heat generation so one part of the computer doesn't get too hot.

Virtual Memory (Paging)

Applications these days take a lot of memory. What happens if your computer runs out of available RAM? Does it hang the system? Not so! Every computer has active memory management that monitors the amount of storage required for uninterrupted operation of the computer. If the RAM is full, the computer declares a portion of the hard disk as a virtual memory section and uses it as extended RAM (or virtual cache). The process is called pagination. Of course, this section is slower than the actual RAM, but helps keep applications ready for access. The user can control how much hard disk space can be used for virtual memory.

Mathematical Concepts

As we have stated before, computers are physical manifestations of several mathematical concepts. Mathematics are the scientific language of solving problems. Over the centuries, mathematicians have theoretically solved many complex issues. Mathematics includes concepts like algebra and geometry.

Number Systems

Mathematics is a game of number manipulation which makes number systems at the center stage of mathematical concepts. There are several different types of number systems. Before we take a look at the number systems, we have to understand the concept of coding.

Coding

A way to represent values using symbols is called coding. Coding is as old as humans. Before the number systems we use today, there were other systems to represent values and messages. An example of coding from ancient times is the Egyptian hieroglyphs.

Number systems are also examples of coding because values are represented using special symbols.

There are different types of number systems, and we are going to discuss a few relevant ones.

Binary System

A binary system has only two symbols, 1 and 0 which are referred to as bits. All the numbers are represented by combining these two symbols. Binary systems are ideal for electronic devices because they also have only two states, on or off. In fact, all electronic devices are based on the binary number system. The number system is positional which means the position of symbols determines the final value. Since there are two symbols in this system, the system has a base of 2.

The sole purpose of input and output systems is to convert data to and from binary system to a form that makes better sense to the user. The first bit from the left side is called Most Significant Bit (MSB) while the first bit from the right is called the Least Significant Bit (LSB).

Here is the binary equivalent code of "this is a message":

01110100 01101000 01101001 01110011 00100000 01101001 01110011 00100000
01100001 00100000 01101101 01100101 01110011 01110011 01100001 01100111
01100101

Decimal System

The decimal system has ten symbols, the numbers 0 through 9. This is also a positional number system where the position of symbols changes the value it represents. All the numbers in this system are created with different combinations of the initial ten symbols. This system has a base 10.

This is also called the Hindu-Arabic number system. Decimals make more sense to humans and are used in daily life. There are two reasons for that.

1. Creating large numbers from the base symbols follows a consistent pattern
2. Performing arithmetic operations in a decimal system is easier compared to other systems

Hexadecimal System

The hexadecimal number system is the only one that has letters as symbols. It has the 10 symbols of the decimal system plus the six alphabets A, B, C, D, E and F. This is also a positional number system with a base 16.

Hexadecimal system is extensively used to code instructions in assembly language.

Number System Conversion

We can convert the numbers from one system to another. There are various online tools to do that. Python also offers number conversion, but it is better to learn how it is done manually.

Binary to Decimal

Here's a binary number 01101001, let's convert it to a decimal number.

$(01101001)_2 = 0 \times 2^7 + 1 \times 2^6 + 1 \times 2^5 + 0 \times 2^4 + 1 \times 2^3 + 0 \times 2^2 + 0 \times 2^1 + 1 \times 2^0$

$(01101001)_2 = 0 + 64 + 32 + 0 + 8 + 0 + 0 + 1$

$(01101001)_2 = (105)_{10}$

Decimal to Binary

To convert a decimal number to binary, we have to repeatedly divide the number by two until the quotient becomes one. Recording the remainder generated at each division step gives us the binary equivalent of the decimal number.

2	105	
2	52	1
2	26	0
2	13	0
2	6	1
2	3	0
	1	1

$$(105)_{10} = (1101001)_2$$

An interesting thing to note here is that $(01101001)_2$ and $(1101001)_2$ represent the same decimal number $(105)_{10}$. It means that just like decimal number system, leading zeros can be ignored in the binary number system.

Binary to Hexadecimal

Binary numbers can be converted to hexadecimal equivalents using two methods.

1. Convert the binary number to decimal, then decimal to hexadecimal number
2. Break binary number in groups of four bits and convert each to its hexadecimal equivalent, keeping the groups' positions in the original binary number intact.

Let's convert $(1101001)_2$ to a hexadecimal number using the second method. The first step is to break the binary number into different groups each of four bits. If the MSB group has less than four bits, make it four by adding leading zeros. Grouping starts from the LSB. So, $(1101001)_2$ will give us $(1001)_2$ and $(0110)_2$. Now, remembering their position in the original binary number, we are going to convert each group to a hexadecimal equivalent.

Here is the table of hexadecimal equivalents of four-bit binary numbers.

Binary	Hexadecimal
0000	0
0001	1
0010	2

0011	3
0100	4
0101	5
0110	6
0111	7
1000	8
1001	9
1010	A
1011	B
1100	C
1101	D
1110	E
1111	F

From the table, we can see $(1001)_2$ is $(9)_{16}$ and $(0110)_2$,the MSB group, is $(6)_{16}$.

Therefore, $(1101001)_2 = (01101001)_2 = (69)_{16}$

Hexadecimal to binary

We can use the above given table to quickly convert hexadecimal numbers to binary equivalents. Let's convert $(4EA9)_{16}$ to binary.

$(4)_{16} = (0100)_2$

$(E)_{16} = (1110)_2$

$(A)_{16} = (1010)_2$

$(9)_{16} = (1001)_2$

So, $(4EA9)_{16} = (0100111010101001)_2 = (100111010101001)_2$

Decimal to Hexadecimal

You can say hexadecimal is an extended version of decimals. Let's convert $(45781)_{10}$ to decimal. But, first, we have to remember this table.

Decimal	Hexadecimal
0	0
1	1
2	2
3	3
4	4
5	5
6	6
7	7
8	8
9	9

10	A
11	B
12	C
13	D
14	E
15	F

We are going to divide the decimal number repeatedly by 16 and record the remainders. The final hexadecimal equivalent is formed by replacing remainder decimals with their correct hexadecimal symbols.

16	45781	
16	2861	5
16	178	13
	11	2

$$(45781)_{10} = (B2D5)_2$$

Hexadecimal to Decimal

Let's convert $(4EA9)_{16}$ to its decimal equivalent.

$(4EA9)_{16} = 4 \times 16^3 + 14 \times 16^2 + 10 \times 16^1 + 9 \times 16^0$

$(4EA9)_{16} = 16384 + 3584 + 160 + 9$

$(4EA9)_{16} = (20137)_{10}$

There's another number system, the octal system, where the number of unique symbols include 0, 1, 2, 3, 4, 5, 6, along with 7. These were developed for small scale devices that worked on small values with limited resources. With the rapid advancements in storage and other computer resources, octal system became insufficient and thus was discarded in favor of hexadecimal number system. You might still find an old octal based computer system.

Fractions (Floating Points)

Decimal number system supports a decimal point '.' to represent portion/slices of a value. For example, if we want to say half of milk bag is empty using numbers, we can write 0.5 or ½ of milk bag is empty. Do other number systems support decimal point? Yes, they do. Let's see how to convert $(0.75)_{10}$ or $(¾)_{10}$ to binary.

¾ x 2 = 6/4 = 1 . (2/4)

2/4 x 2 = 4/4 = 1

$(0.75)_{10} = (¾)_{10} = (.11)_2$

Negatives

In the decimal system, a dash or hyphen '-' is placed before a number to declare it as a negative. There are different ways to denote negative numbers in the binary system. The easiest is to consider the MSB as a sign bit, which means if MSB is 1, the number is negative and if the MSB is 0, the number is positive. Determining if a hexadecimal number is negative or positive is a bit tricky. The easiest way is to convert the number into binary and perform the checks for negatives in binary system.

Linear Algebra

Did you hate algebra in school? I have some bad news for you! Linear algebra is heavily involved in programming because it's one of the best mathematical ways to solve problems. According to Wikipedia, algebra is the study of mathematical symbols and the rules for manipulating these symbols. The field advanced thanks to the works of Muhammad ibn Musa al-Khwarizmi who introduced the reduction and balancing methods and treated algebra as an independent field of mathematics. Algebra comes from (al-jabr) in the name of the book al-Kitāb al-mukhtaṣar fī ḥisāb al-jabr wal-muqābala (The Compendious Book on Calculation by Completion (al-jabr) and Balancing (*al-muqābala*)) Khwarizmi wrote on the subject. During that era, the concept of 'x' and 'y' etc. variable notation wasn't widespread but during the Islamic Golden Age, Arabs had a fondness of lengthy "layman terms" descriptions of problems and solutions and that is what Khwarizmi explained algebra concepts in his book. The book dealt with many practical real-life problems including the fields of finance, planning, and legal.

So, we know what algebra is. But, where does "linear" comes from? For that, we have to understand what a linear system is. It is a mathematical model where the system attributes (variables) have a linear relation among themselves. The easiest way to explain this is if the plot between system attributes is a straight line, the system is linear. Linear systems are much simpler than the nonlinear systems. The set of algebraic concepts that relate to linear systems is referred to as linear algebra. Linear algebra helps resolve system problems such as missing attribute values. The first step is to create linear equations to establish the relationship between the system variables.

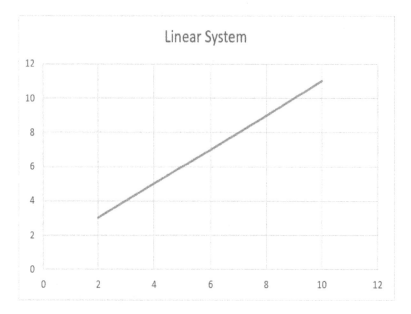

Statistics

Another important field of mathematics that is crucial in various computer science applications. Data analysis and machine learning wouldn't be what they are without the advancements made in statistical concepts during the 20th century. Let's see some concepts related to statistics.

Outlier

Outlier detection is very important in statistical analysis. It helps in homogenizing the sample data. After detecting the outliers, what to do with them is crucial because they directly affect the analysis results. There are many possibilities including:

Discarding Outlier

Sometimes it's better to discard outliers because they have been recorded due to some error. This usually happens where the behaviour of the system is already known.

System Malfunction

But, outliers can also indicate a system malfunction. It is always better to investigate the outliers instead of discarding them straightaway.

Average

Finding the center of a data sample is crucial in statistical analysis because it reveals a lot of system characteristics. There are different types of averages, each signifying something important.

Mean

Mean is the most common average. All the data values are added and divided by the number of data values added together. For example, you sell shopping bags to a well-renowned grocery store and they want to know how much each shopping bag can carry. You completely fill 5 shopping bags with random grocery items and weigh them. Here are the readings in pounds.

5.5, 6.0, 4.95, 7.1, 5.0

You calculate the mean as (5.5 + 6 + 4.95 + 7.1 + 5) / 5 = 5.71. You can tell the grocery store your grocery bags hold 5.71 lbs on average.

Median

Median is the center value with respect to the position of data in a sample data when it's sorted in ascending order. If sample data has odd members, the median is the value with an equal number of values on both flanks. If sample data has an even number of values, the median is calculated by finding the mean of two values in the middle with equal number of items on both sides.

Mode

Mode is the most recurring value in a dataset. If there is no recurring value in the sample data, there is no mode.

Variance

To find how much each data value in a sample data changes with respect to the average of the sample data, we calculate the variance. Here is a general formula to calculate variance.

sum of (each data point - mean of sample points $)^2$ / number of data points in the sample.

If the variance is low in a sample data, it means there are no outliers in the data.

Standard Deviation

We take the square root of variance to find standard deviation. This relates the mean of sample data to the whole of sample data.

Probability

No one can accurately tell what will happen in the future. We can only predict what is going to happen with some degree of certainty. The probability of an event is written mathematically as,

Probability = number of possible ways an event can happen / total number of possibilities

A few points:

1. Probability can never be negative
2. Probability ranges between one and zero
3. To calculate probability, we assume that the set of events we are working with occur independently without any interference.

Finding the probability of an event can change the probability of something happening in a subsequent event. It depends upon how we are interacting with the system to find event probabilities.

Distribution

There are many types of distributions. In this book, whenever we talk about distribution, we refer to probability distribution unless explicitly stated otherwise. Let's take an example of flipping coins and see what is the distribution of such events.

H H H	T H H
H H T	H T T
H T H	T H T
T T T	T T H

This is a very simple event with only a handful of possible outcomes. We can easily determine the probability of different outcomes. But, this is almost impossible in complex systems with thousands or millions of possible outcomes. Distributions work much better in such cases by visually representing the probability curve. It makes more sense than looking at a huge table of fractions or small decimal numbers.

We call a probability distribution discrete if we know all the possible outcomes beforehand.

Chapter 2: Introduction to Python

Before doing anything else, visit https://www.python.org/. The website contains all Python standard packages and comprehensive documentation. Here's a problem: official documentations are written for professional programmers and it doesn't make sense for beginners. This is where Python beats the competition: the huge community of volunteers and contributors who have created so much learning material that's ideal for beginners. This book is also part of that learning material.

Why Python?

Almost everyone who starts learning programming questions the choices they made before, like why did I pick this language? Why I am learning programming? If you went with Python because it's the trend, we can assure you that you have made a correct decision. Python is a high-level language built for beginners. From the start, the language instils the concept of arranged, clean code in the minds of a programmer. In other languages, you spend considerable time learning the syntax. But with Python, you learn how to program without worrying too much about the specific syntax. It doesn't mean there is no specific syntax to follow, it means there are less things to worry about.

The programming language is open-source which means more people have access to it. You will find tutorials on almost everything there is to do in Python. I still remember the last few months of my college days when I was stuck with my final project. I had tried everything I could think of for days but there was no progress. I started searching on the Internet and after some more worryful hours, I stumbled upon the work of another student who had solved a similar issue. I modified his approach to my requirements and voila, my project was complete! I am very sure that if I had been working with a proprietary platform, I would have failed that course.

Remembering this, I should tell you an important skill that you should master before you start learning programming. The skill is to become an advanced user of search engines. No matter which search engine you use, Google, Bing, Yahoo, etc., you must know all or most of the tips and tricks on how to find something online. There is a high chance someone has already gone through what you are trying to do, or has done something similar. You will feel like a hacker once you master the art of using search engines!

Basic Stuff

Constants

Constants are symbols that already have fixed value in the programming language. As the name suggests, you cannot change constants. Constants have specific data type. For example, number 21 is a constant.

Expressions

Expressions will most frequently appear on the right hand side of an operator and can be a combination of constants, variables, and more operators. When writing a script, an expression will not result in any output unless the result of expression is either stored in a variable or used to make a decision.

Operators

A wide range of operators are supported by Python. Operators are commands/instructions that perform specific operation on the data supplied with the operators which are themselves called operands. Here's a list of some important operators in Python.

Arithmetic Operators

Arithmetics is another vital part of mathematics and Python supports a long list of arithmetic operations. Here are some examples.

Operator	Meaning

+ Perform addition of operands - order of operands doesn't matter

- Perform subtraction of one operand from the other (right side from the left side)

• Multiply operands and their order doesn't affect the output

/ Divide one operand from the other (left side by the right side) and returns the quotient

% Divides one operand from the other (left side by the right side) but returns the remainder

** Returns exponents of an operand

Comparative Operators

These operators are vital for conditional statements. The below table contains some examples.

Operator	Meaning

== Check if two operands are equal

!= Check if two operands are not equal

➢ Check if the left side operand is greater than the right side operand

< Check if the left side operand is

less than the right side operand

Logical Operators

We can perform multiple operations together and see the combined effect

Operator	Meaning
and	performs logical AND operation
	- only true if all operands are true
or	performs logical OR operation
	- only false if all operands are false
not	reverse the result
	of a logical operation

Assignment Operator

The only operator that lets you store

information, the '=' operator, is very

crucial to Python programming. On the

left side is always the variable name,

and on the right side is a constant,

expression, or a function

that returns a value.

Python executes operators according

to the PEMDAS rule of precedence.

Here is the summary.

1. Anything wrapped with
    parentheses will be executed first.

    If you want to execute

    an operation first by ignoring

    its precedence, put them

    inside parentheses.

2. Exponent operator has the
    next highest precedence.

3. The next precedence is
    shared by multiplication

    and division operations

4. Last but not least, addition

    and subtraction have the same

    precedence and are executed

    at the very end

If more than one operators have

the same precedence, Python will

execute the operator that's at the

leftmost side of the expression.

Here are a few practical examples.

```
>>>4+(8*(3-1))+(12*2)
44
>>> 9183 % 21
6
>>>mon=767
>>>mon*(mon/mon)
767.0
```

Variables

You can store constants or results

gathered through a function return

or expression result in a variable.

In Python, we do not have to pre-declare

the type of variable. The type of data

stored in the variable determines its type.

```
a =4
print a
```

We stored the integer '4' in the variable 'a'.

It makes the variable 'a' of the integer type.

There are different rules you need

to follow when creating a variable name.

1. The first character of a variable
   name must be an alphabet

2. Numbers can be used in a variable name

3 You can capitalize the first
name of a variable name

but it's not considered good practice

4 Both uppercase and lowercase

alphabets can be used in

a variable name

5 Underscore '_' is the only

special character allowed

in a variable name

Python has 31 keywords in total that

you cannot use as a variable name

. Here's the complete list for reference.

1. global
2. if
3. import
4. in
5. is
6. lambda
7. not
8. or
9. pass

10. print
11. raise
12. return
13. try
14. while
15. with
16. yield
17. and
18. as
19. assert
20. break
21. class
22. continue
23. def
24. del
25. elif
26. else
27. except
28. exec
29. finally
30. for
31. from

A few examples of assigning variables are below

sTr = "Howdy partner!" #string variable

fLt = 3.14 # floating variable

sTRng = "3.14" #double quotes mean its a string

To check the type of variable, we can use the type() method.

type(sTRng)

You will see the following output.

<type 'str'>

Statements

All the instructions that you give to Python are called statements. Statements may or may not produce an output. When you write a script, you are sequencing a number of statements for the Python interpreter to execute one by one.

Test the following lines of code using Python.

i = 411

i = i + 27

print i

We are doing something unique here. We know that in Python, the right side of the operator '=', which is "i + 27" is calculated first and the result is assigned to the variable name 'i' on the left. Using this knowledge, we have overwritten the value of variable 'i' with a new value.

End of statements

Most programming languages were inspired from the C language, hence use the semicolon ';' to mark the end of a statement. Python, although based on the C language, deviated from this practice and used newlines and tabs to demarcate code blocks. It increased readability but creates problem when copy pasting codes.

If you want to write a single line of code to take two lines on your screen, you can use a backward slash '\'. Here's an example.

```
>>> breKK = \
... 971 + \
... 412
```

The three dots indicate the Python interpreter is waiting for the next part of the code. You will see this when writing a loop, conditional or function code block. Checking the value of variable "breKK" will tell if the program ran correctly. The returned value should be 1383.

```
>>> breKK
1383
```

Conditionals

We use conditionals to check a condition and direct the flow of the program execution. These statements are integral to deploying the concept of control flow in Python.

The if statement

If the given condition is true, execute the next block of code otherwise ignore it.

```
>>> num = 77
>>> if num == 18:
...             print("Execute this")
...
>>>
```

There's no output because the print statement never got executed because the condition "if num == 18" returned false. The indented blocks are referred to as suites. In case the if condition is true, the print statement will be executed. The following code gives the output of "Execute this".

```
>>> num = 77
>>> if num == 77:
```

```
...          print("Execute this")

...
```

Execute this

```
>>>
```

We can combine the "if" statement with the "else" statement to execute codes in case the "if" condition returns false.

```
>>> vaRa = 47

>>> if vaRa < 23:

...          print("vaRa is less")

... else:

...          print("vaRa is more")

...
```

vaRa is more

```
>>>
```

The variable "vaRA" is assigned the value of 47. The "if" condition returns false which directs the control flow to the code block under "else" statement for execution. We can use elif to check a condition before executing a code block.

```
>>> vaRa = 47

>>> if vaRa < 23:

...          print("vaRa is less")

... elif xcon > 33:

...          print("vaRa is more")

... else:

...          print("undetermined")

...
```

vaRa is more

>>>

Here's an example of nesting multiple "if" statements.

```
>>> ynst = 991
>>> znet = "Tssp"
>>> if znet == "Tssp":
...         if ynst > 200:
...         print("ynst out of range")
...         elif ynst < 100:
...         print("ynst too low")
...         else:
...         print("ynst within range")
... else:
...         print("out of scope")
...
```

ynst within range

As stated earlier, we can combine multiple checks inside an "if" statement using logical operators.

```
>>> ynst = 147
>>> znet = "Test"
>>> if znet == "Result" and ynst == 147:
...         print("Sweet!")
... else:
...         print("Bummer!")
```

...

Bummer!

The "znet == "Result"" check will always return false because znet is assigned the value "Tssp". The "and" operator returns true only if all operations return true which was not the case this time.

Here is another thing that makes Python stand out from other programming languages: it has no switch-case statement. Truth be told, if you properly master if-else-elif, you will never miss the switch-case statement.

Loops

Humans hate repetitive work. It's boring. However, computers excel at performing the same task over and over again. There are two major types of loops in Python: the "for" and "while" loops.

The for loop

The "for" loop is ideal if you know how many times the loop needs to be executed. Let's discuss the things you must know before working with "for" loops.

Iterable

These loops require an entity that offers multiple attributes that the loop can use to iterate over.

Iterator

The loop also requires a pointer like entity that will go over the iterable. Depending upon the iterable, the iterator stores iterable entity's data while iterating.

A simple "for" loop example is below.

```
>>> for itr in range(190,200):
...         print i
...
190
191
```

192

193

194

195

196

197

198

199

A simple program, but it highlights a few very important things.

1. range() creates a sequence of numbers starting and ending in the limits given to the method
2. The "for" loop executes as soon as the maximum limit is reached and not when it's crossed. This is evident from the program output as the loop execution stopped as soon as the value of "itr" became 100.

The range() method has a default increment of one but you can change that. But, a point to remember, only integers can be given to the range().

```
>>> for xyz in range(22,33,2):
...         print(xyz)
...
22
24
26
28
20
32
```

The range() will work even if we omit the lower limit but we can't pass a step also. For example:

```
>>> for nUm in range(7):

...         print(nUm)

...

0

1

2

3

4

5

6

7
```

An important observation here is the number started from zero which is very valuable when using range() to output indices for data structures.

Here's a question: will we get an error if we use a lower limit less than the upper limit? Let's test it out.

```
>>> for per in range(100, 50):

...         print(per)

...

>>>
```

Interestingly, no errors were given. The loop just didn't execute.

The while loop

When we do not know how many times a loop needs to iterate, we use the "while" loop. At the start of each iteration, the condition is checked and the loop block is executed if the condition is still true. This property makes it ideal to create infinite loops which are very important in various applications such as game development.

```
>>> itr = 91
```

```
>>> while (itr < 95):

...         print("Executing this statement")

...         itr = itr + 1 # can also write as itr += 1

...
```

Executing this statement

Executing this statement

Executing this statement

Executing this statement

As you can see, we have to explicitly update the "itr" variable because "while" only checks the condition. If we comment out the itr = itr + 1, we will end up with an infinite loop because value of "itr" will never become greater than 95.

"While" loops should be used with extreme care and only when you are confident with your programming skills.

Data Structures in Python

Lists

Up till now, we have seen variables that can hold one value at a time. In many cases, this is insufficient. For example, you want to store the hour marks and the task you need to do in a list.

tasklist = ['8.00','wake up', '9.00', 'work', '13.00', 'lunch', '17.00', 'off to home']

All the values in the "tasklist" are strings but we can combine different types of data in a list. The first item index of a list is always zero. Let's test that theory.

```
>>> tasklist[0]
```

'8.00'

The len() function provides the number of items in a list.

```
>>> len(tasklist)
```

8

Lists are iterables hence we can use loops to go over them. Let's use a "for" loop to access all the items in our "tasklist".

```
>>> for tsk in tasklist:
...         print tsk
...
8.00
wake up
9.00
work
13.00
lunch
17.00
off to home
```

The operator "in" is used to get one item from the list at every loop iteration. We can use an index to get a list item. Can we know the index if we have an item value? Yes we can, and here's an example.

```
>>> for tsk in tasklist:
...         print("Value:",tsk,"- Position:",tasklist.index(tsk))
...
Value: 8.00 - Position: 0
Value: wake up - Position: 1
Value: 9.00 - Position: 2
Value: work - Position: 3
Value: 13.00 - Position: 4
```

Value: lunch - Position: 5

Value: 17.00 - Position: 6

Value: off to home - Position: 7

Lists support negative values as index. For example, to get the last value of a list, we can use a negative one as index.

```
>>> print(implist[-1])
```

off to home

It is possible to replace data in a list.

```
>>> tasklist[2] = "Now it's 9am"
```

```
>>> print(tasklist)
```

['8.00','wake up', 'Now it's 9am', 'work', '13.00', 'lunch', '17.00', 'off to home']

We can verify the membership of an item in a list.

```
>>> if "sleep" not in implist:
...         print("sleep is for the weak")
...
```

sleep is for the weak

The list method of append() can be used to add new items to the list. The new item is added at the end of the list.

```
>>>tasklist.append("dinner")
```

```
>>> tasklist
```

['8.00','wake up', 'Now it's 9am', 'work', '13.00', 'lunch', '17.00', 'off to home', 'dinner']

We can use the insert() method to add an item at a specific index position.

```
>>> tasklist.insert(8,"19.00")
```

```
>>> tasklist
```

['8.00','wake up', 'Now it's 9am', 'work', '13.00', 'lunch', '17.00', 'off to home', '19.00', 'dinner']

We can remove a specific item using its value through the remove() method.

>>> tasklist.remove("19.00")

>>> tasklist

['8.00','wake up', 'Now it's 9am', 'work', '13.00', 'lunch', '17.00', 'off to home', 'dinner']

We can remove a specific item using its position with the pop() method.

>>> tasklist.pop(8)

"dinner"

>>> tasklist

['8.00','wake up', 'Now it's 9am', 'work', '13.00', 'lunch', '17.00', 'off to home']

In case no index is provided, pop() removes the last item in the list. So, in the above code we could have gotten the same result by not providing the index '8' in the pop().

The extend() method is one of the many ways to join two lists.

>>> funlist = ["weekend","24/7 fun", "no work"]

>>> tasklist.extend(funlist)

>>> tasklist

['8.00','wake up', 'Now it's 9am', 'work', '13.00', 'lunch', '17.00', 'off to home', "weekend","24/7 fun", "no work"]

All the items from "funlist" are added at the end of "tasklist".

You can nest lists as well which means a list can contain other lists.

>>> newlist = [tasklist, funlist]

Dictionaries

A dictionary is an advanced form of arrays because we can set custom index (called key) for each item (called value) in it. The key and value can be of any data type.

You can change the contents of a dictionary. A dictionary can hold another dictionary.

Let's rewrite our tasklist as a dictionary. You will immediately see the data make more sense.

```
>>> taskDict = {

... "8.00": "wake up",

... "9.00": "work",

... "13.00": "lunch",

... "17.00": "off to home"

... }
```

Instead of a numerical index, we use the key to retrieve a value.

```
>>> taskDict["9.00"]

work
```

To know how many key-value pairs are present in a dictionary, we can use the len().

```
>>> len(taskDict)

4
```

We can also get all the keys in a dictionary using the method keys() which returns a list containing all the keys.

```
>>> taskDict.keys()

['8.00', '9.00', '13.00', '17.00']
```

In a similar way, the values() method returns all the values in a dictionary as a list.

```
>>> taskDict.values()
```

['wake up', 'work', 'lunch', 'off to home']

Let's add a list to this dictionary.

>>> taskDict["Fun List"] = ["weekend","24/7 fun", "no work"]

"Fun List" is the key. Dictionaries have become ordered in Python 3.0+ that make them even faster and newly added items are always added at the end of a dictionary.

The pop() method is also supported by dictionaries.

>>> taskDict.pop("Fun List")

["weekend","24/7 fun", "no work"]

The operator "in" is applicable to dictionaries too but it works slightly different. For dictionaries, the "in" operator retrieves the keys. We can use it with a loop to retrieve the keys and values of any dictionary.

>>> for timeMarc in taskDict:

...   print("Time:", timeMarc,"- Task:",taskDict[timeMarc])

...

Time: 8.00 - Task: wake up

Time: 9.00 - Task: work

Time: 13.00 - Task: lunch

Time: 17.00 - Task: off to home

The "in" operator along with the conditional "if" statement can be used to check if certain data is present as a key in a dictionary.

>>> if "22.00" in taskDict:

...   print("you should be asleep by now!")

... else:

...   print("good boy")

...

good boy

To find something in the values, we can replace taskDict() with taskDict().values()

```
>>> if "sleep" in taskDict.values():

...          print("sleep is good!")

... else:

...          print("sleep is for the weak!")

...
```

sleep is for the weak!

We can add a dictionary inside another dictionary.

```
>>> newDict = {

... "a": "apple",

... "b": "ball",

... "c": "cat",

... "d": "door",

... "vowels": {'one': 'a', 'two': 'e', 'three': 'i', 'four': 'o', 'five': 'u'},

... }
```

Tuples

Tuples don't serve any purpose other than to provide a medium when we are required to pass information between system layers or components without the chance of change.

Here's our first tuple.

```
>>> tasktup = ('8.00','wake up', '9.00', 'work', '13.00', 'lunch', '17.00', 'off to home')

>>> print(tasktup)
```

('8.00','wake up', '9.00', 'work', '13.00', 'lunch', '17.00', 'off to home')

Python allows you to change the type of a variable. For example str(64) will convert it into '64'. We can use the same concept to change a tuple. We first convert the tuple to a list, make the edits, and convert the updated list back to a tuple.

```
>>> templist = list(tasktup )

>>> templist.pop()

'off to home'

>>> templist.insert(8,"overtime")

>>> tasktupnew = tuple(templist)

>>> tasktupnew
```

('8.00','wake up', '9.00', 'work', '13.00', 'lunch', '17.00', 'overtime')

Sets

Python has maintained the rules of mathematical set theory when creating its "sets" data structure.

```
>>> taskset = set(['8.00','wake up', '9.00', 'work', '13.00', 'lunch', '17.00', 'off to home'])
```

Since the sets are unordered, there's no index. Therefore, you cannot change items in a set using an index value, but you can add new items or remove existing ones.

We can use all the other methods we have learned so far and also some more such as add() and update(). Both add new elements at the end of the set. You are already familiar with the remove() and discard() and both are supported by sets.

Chapter 3: Shifting Gears

Python is very extendable, thanks to the hundreds of external libraries written by volunteer contributors. In this chapter, we are going to work with some of the external libraries, how to install and import them, and use the methods available in those libraries.

External Libraries

We are going to use the popular chart creation "matplotlib" library as a means of demonstrating how to install and import an external library.

We can use pip to install matplotlib. Open the Windows command prompt and run the following command. A note here: If you are using an advanced interpreter like PyCharm, the command prompt is accessible from the interpreter. You do not have to open command prompt separately.

pip install matplotlib

Python will download and install the library and all the required resources. Once it is setup, we can import the library to start using it.

import matplotlib.pyplot as plt

When we ask Python to import a library or your own written module, there is a path registry that Python searches to find that resource. The following code will give you all the paths registered in the registry.

>>> import sys

>>> for resourcePath in sys.path:

...   print(resourcePath)

...

You can import your own script in another script. Place your script in one of the paths the above code outputs and you will be able to use "import" to use it in another script.

The import process takes a lot of resources and can make your interpreter or entire computer become unresponsive. Do not worry, just give it a minute, the process will finish and everything will be back to normal. If you are running in interactive mode and there's no output, it means the import was a success. Otherwise, there will be an error.

Because the import process takes too many resources, it's only run once for each resource. Duplicate import for the same library/module is ignored.

import datetime

import datetime

In the above two import statements, only the first one will run. Python will not execute the second statement. It means you cannot recursively call your module just like you can recursively call a function to do something. If the module/library has various functions (methods), we can import a specific one just like we did with the matplotlib.pyplot. Once imported, we can start using it.

>>> plt.plot([10, 13, 15, 17])

[<matplotlib.lines.Line2D object at 0x000001905095FF88>]

The pyplot is a simple line chart or line graph. If you look closely, we have given coordinates using the plot() function.

>>> plt.ylabel("Y Coordinates")

Text(0,0.5,u'Y Coordinates')

>>> plt.xlabel("X Coordinates")

Text(0.5,0,u'X Coordinates')

>>> plt.style.use('grayscale')

The "Text" outputs are just a confirmation that the axes labels are updated to the new values. To view the plot, we use the show() method.

>>> plt.show()

The plot is shown in a new window. It looks like below.

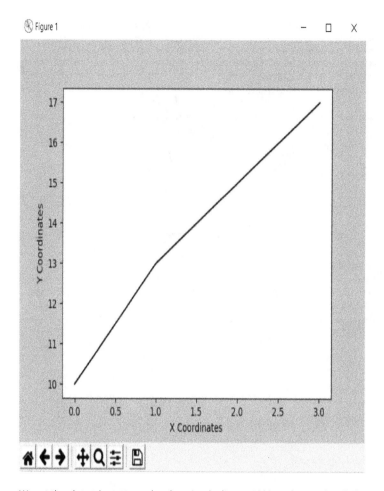

We set the plot style as grayscale otherwise the line would have been colored. There are different tools available to edit or save this plot. The plot remains open until you close it using the close button. This is important because the interactive mode might be unresponsive until you close the graph.

The matplotlib library is a huge resource to visualize data in many different ways. It's not possible to cover it completely in this book. We used it as an example for importing and using an external library. Later on, we will use another library to create graphs and plots.

Strings

Python supports extreme string manipulation. The language considers strings as a data structure, specifically a list of characters. This enables the programmer to manipulate strings in ways not possible in other programming languages. The advanced methods make Python also better for data analysis where the data is string most of the time. Data type conversion is also very straightforward. Python handles all string operations faster than the competition.

```
>>> op = "974"
```

```
>>> type(op)
```

```
<class 'str'>
```

```
>>> pp = 'this is string'
```

```
>>> type(op)
```

```
<class 'str'>
```

Enclose anything in single or double quotes for Python to consider it as string type. Notice how Python returned "class". This has changed in recent Python versions so the language has become more uniform with the statement "Everything in Python is a class."

```
>>> strJ = op + pp
```

```
>>> print(strJ)
```

```
974this is string
```

The '+' operator acts as a concatenator for strings. We can also use the join() method to concatenate strings.

```
>>> strJ = op.join(pp)
```

```
>>> print(strJ)
```

```
t974h974i974s974 974i974s974 974s974t974r974i974n974g
```

The output is a little weird and unexpected but this is just how join() method works. The result looks more like a multiplication of both strings. The join() method breaks the argument string into individual elements and joins the string the method is applied to with those individual elements.

```
>>> str(00457)
```

```
File "<stdin>", line 1

 xx = 00457

    ^
```

SyntaxError: invalid token

In newer Python versions, we cannot put leading zeros, it gives a syntax error. There's a work around though: the zfill() method.

```
>>> str(457).zfill(6)
```

'000457'

The zfill() method is only applicable on strings, so we need to convert the number to string before adding the leading zeroes. There are already three digits in 457 so we gave six as zfill() argument because we want to add three leading zeros making the total characters in the string six.

The len() works on the string the same way it works on other data structures - it gives the number of elements.

```
>>> exStr = "139 characters"
```

```
>>> len(exStr)
```

13

Combine len() with range() and we can dissect the string to access each character individually.

```
>>> for chr in range(len(exStr)):

...         print(exStr[chr], end=' ')

...
```

1 3 9   c h a r a c t e r s

Some observations.

1. Just like lists, we can access the string using its index
2. To stop Python from adding a newline after the print output, we have added a comma ',' which adds a space instead of a newline

There are several ways to access the elements of a string. Let's try another method that uses the 'in' operator.

```
>>> for chr in exStr:
...         print(chr)
...
```

139 characters

Fewer characters to get the exact same output. The first character has the index zero, as proven by the example below.

```
>>> exStr[0]
```

'1'

The last element has an index which is one less than the length of the string.

```
>>> exStr[len(exStr)-1]
```

's'

All this information can be used to utilize a while() loop.

```
>>> ind = 0
>>> while ind <= len(exStr) - 1:
...         print(exStr[ind])
...         ind = ind + 1
...
```

139 characters

In the while loop, we could have wrapped "len(exStr) - 1" within parentheses but it isn't required for our current example.

Slice and Dice Strings

Slicing a string is very easy using the indices. Slicing creates a new string from the string.

string[start index:optional stop index:optional step amount]

Let us have this slicing technique applied to the exStr string.

```
>>> exStr[4:]
```

'haracters'

Since we did not provide a stopping index, the returned string has all the characters from the starting index to the end of the original string. The easiest way to reverse a string is to use slicing without the start and stop indices and use a step value of negative one.

```
>>> longstr[::-1]
```

'sretcarahc 31'

Extraction and Replacement of Substrings

The creators of Python have tried their best to have Python make sense in every way possible. The method names almost always closely resemble their application. Let's focus on the string method split(), which splits the string according to the given substring.

```
>>> exStr.split()
```

['13', 'characters']

Since we didn't provide any argument to split(), the default value of space ' ' was used. This is apparent from the example below.

```
>>> 'kajhskjdha'.split()
```

['kajhskjdha']

Let's provide a substring.

```
>>> 'kajhskjdha'.split('a')
```

['k', 'jhskjdh', '']

The returned list of strings do not have the argument we used to split the string. We can also replace a portion of a string with something else.

```
>>> exStr.replace("13","some")
```

'some characters'

Note that replace() doesn't change the real string. We can definitely check the contents of exStr.

```
>>> exStr
```

'13 characters'

The replace() by default replaces all the instances of a specific substring with the required substring.

```
>>> exStr.replace('a','e', 1)
```

'13 cheracters'

Not just a single character, replace can be used to replace entire words or phrases with something new. You might have used the find and replace tool on many software applications that deal with text such as word processors. Notice how easy it is to implement such as feature using the replace() method. Maybe a future challenge could be to develop a word processing application using Python?

Exceptional Handling

Error Types

There are two main categories of errors in Python.

Syntax errors

When you do not follow the rules of script writing in Python, you will get a syntax error, also called parsing error. We have already seen an example of syntax/parsing error.

```
>>> str(00457)
  File "<stdin>", line 1
    xx = 00457
         ^
SyntaxError: invalid token
```

Whenever an error occurs, Python tries to provide an explanation so the programmer knows what needs to be fixed. The explanation and hints are sometimes not very easy to understand but most of the time, you should consider the hints carefully.

Exceptions

If you make no mistakes in syntax during the program writing, you might still end up having the wrong output or breaking program flow with an error. Let us discuss some more errors.

Index error

Using an index that is not present in a data structure will lead to an index error.

>>> listrand = ["python","the","best", "programming", "language"]

>>> listrand[100]

IndexError: list index out of range

Name error

If we use a resource without assigning a value to it first, we get an error.

>>> listrand = ["python","the","best", "programming", "language"]

>>> print(listrandom)

NameError: name 'listrandom' is not defined

Type error

When we try to perform an operation that is not supported by the given data, it leads to a type error.

>>> intpp = 741

>>> strpp = "007"

>>> strpp + intpp

TypeError: can only concatenate str (not "int") to str

If you apply the arithmetic operator '+' but the position operands is reversed, the explanation of type error becomes different.

```
>>> intpp + strpp
```

```
TypeError: unsupported operand type(s) for +: 'int' and 'str'
```

Import error

If you import a library/module that Python is not able to find in the directories listed in the path directory, you will get an import error.

```
>>> import custmod
```

```
ModuleNotFoundError: No module named 'custmod'
```

```
>>> from math import triag
```

```
ImportError: cannot import name 'triag' from 'math' (unknown location)
```

We see two different descriptions for the same error because the error happened due to different reasons.

Logical error

When you make an error that's not an error for Python but we still don't get the output we were expecting, then we have encountered a logical error. Logical errors are very difficult to find and fix because you do not get any hint as to what's causing it.

Let's write a script with a logical error to illustrate how a logical error can occur. Even with this simple example, it would be a serious task to find the cause of error because it's really not apparent.

```
import math
```

```
num1 = 200
```

```
num2 = num1 / 5 * math.pi
```

```
print num2
```

The following output is generated after saving and executing the above script.

```
125.66370614359172
```

The result is wrong because we were expecting an output of 12.732395447351628. We know that there is something wrong with the program, but we have no idea where the issue is. We will have to deploy troubleshooting techniques to find the problem. We know that Python always follows PEMDAS when calculating the result of an expression containing arithmetic operators. Since multiplication and division have the same priority, Python is going from left to right with the execution. The "num1" is divided by "5" and that result is multiplied by the pi value. We have to use brackets to force Python to executing the problem.

```
num2 = num1 / ( 5 * math.pi )
```

The correct output will be shown now.

```
12.732395447351628
```

Exceptional Handling

All errors, except logical ones, break the execution flow. This is unacceptable if you are creating an application. In earlier days, it used to be very common that an unexpected situation would break the application or system. Thanks to better programming practices now, exceptional handling is now part of all high-level programming languages and all programmers utilize it to create distributable applications. What is exception handling? The technique to handle errors so they don't break the program execution. For example, we know users will enter bad data even though we have given all the instructions. It is always a good idea to wrap the input() statement inside a try-except pair. Even if the data provided by the user is correct, it is very easy to forget that input() takes the input as string. Applying any method or operation on this input that is not compatible with strings will result in an error.

```
>>> try:

...         capT = input('Enter a number: ')

...         res = capT / 2

...         print(res)

... except:

...         print("There is an error in the try block")

...
```

There is an error in the try block

We tried to divide a string and strings do not support division. An error has occurred but because it's in a code that's wrapped with "try", execution flow doesn't break. However, the entire code block is ignored and the code block wrapped with "except" is executed. Hence, the output that we see is "There is an error in the try block".

There is also the "else" wrapper that we can use to execute code block in case the "try" block code doesn't raise an exception. Remember that if there's no error, the "try" also gets executed. Here's an example proof.

```
>>> centRy = 113

>>> try:

...         print(centRy)

... except:

...         print("No exceptions this time")

... else:

...         print(centRy)

...

113

113
```

There's another option, "finally", code wrapped with it which will be executed no matter what the result of the code block inside "try" was.

```
>>> chk = "This value is safely stored."

>>> try:

...         print(chk)

... except:

...         print("Something is wrong")

... finally:

...         print("I will persevere")

...

This value is safely stored.

I will persevere.
```

Best Troubleshooting Practices

In the above section, we saw the simplest possible examples for each type of error. Sometimes even with the Python hint, we do not know what the cause of the error is or how to fix it. This happens because the explanation provided by Python doesn't make sense to us. Let's see our previous example again.

```
>>> str(00457)

 File "<stdin>", line 1

  xx = 00457

    ^

SyntaxError: invalid token
```

We know we have made a mistake, and we also know there is a syntax error. But, we don't know that Python doesn't support leading zeros and that's what is causing the error. "Invalid token" doesn't make sense unless you already know what it means. If you are seeing this error for the first time, you will have to research to understand what has happened and what needs to be changed. As stated before, logical errors are even harder to fix because we have no idea what and where things went wrong. Imagine a script of thousands of lines of code and you are not getting the expected output. What to do next? Where do you start? How do you track the issue smartly so you do not waste more time in troubleshooting than you did coding? There are some best practices when it comes to debugging and troubleshooting.

Planning before execution

There is a reason companies spend more budget and time at planning a particular business venture than actually doing it. All the aspects are carefully analyzed and discussed to remove any loopholes. There are various tools that help here. In programming, we have algorithms (textual) and flowcharts (visual). Both tools should be deployed, but algorithms are usually used before flowcharts because algorithms are system independent. They are used to roughly estimate the process. Flowcharts are much more detailed and easier to understand as they not only show the flow of execution but also the different requirements.

Leave breadcrumbs

Programming is like exploring a huge cave or walking a labyrinth. If you did not leave breadcrumbs to help you back track, you will be lost forever! Comments are useful because most of the time there are multiple people working on the same project and everyone needs to understand what you have written. It also helps you remember what you did when you were coding because, believe me, no one remembers what they did. If you don't remember how you resolved a problem or why you coded a specific way, it's very difficult to update it or correct it.

Dry run

A lost art - this used to the the main troubleshooting method. There are now better tools such as live trackers that you can utilize to see all the changes happening in a program. But, this tradition of using the pen and paper and doing it the hard way has lead to great discoveries. I still prefer that method. There's just something about it that helps me visualize the links between different things and find the problem. Of course, that doesn't work in a script that has thousands of line. For those projects, you definitely need the latest debugging tools.

Test unexpected behaviour

Programmers are problem solvers. They think in a specific mindset but that might not always be how the end user would think or use the product. The best way to make sure your program does not break because the user entered "one" instead of '1' is to unit test the script with millions of different inputs and analyze the result. If the script breaks in certain situations, you can program to fix them.

Debugging in Python

The "pdb" tool is the standard debugging tool in Python and works the same way debuggers work on other platforms. You can add a marker so the debugger would start from there and then execute your code step by step, monitoring all the changes your script makes. Here's a script that we are going to examine with the "pdb" debugger.

```python
import pdb


pdb.set_trace()

num = input("Enter a number: ")

try:

        numAct = inp(num)

except:

        print(type(num))

print('Multiplication table of %d', %num)

for mult in range(1, 21):

        print("%d x %d = %d" % (num, mult, num*mult))
```

A simple multiplication table generator script where the first line has the "pdb.set_trace()" set. Before we could use the tracer, we have to import the "pdb" library. The debugger will start from the very first line. A small window will appear that belongs to the debugger and can take various commands. You can start debugging by passing many commands including the following.

1. (s)tep - execute the line of code debugger is currently positioned at
2. (c)ontinue - execute the remaining code unless a breakpoint is met, in that case stop the execution there
3. (n)ext - works well on functions and executes until a newline is met or until a return is encountered

Use the commands to see how your program changes with the execution of each line.

Functions

Python supports object-oriented programming as well as functional programming. In the latter, programmers can name some lines of code and use that name to run those lines of code as many times as needed. The lines of code defined by a name are called functions. You can also make the function take on arguments which can be passed when calling the function.

```
>>> def prntseq(num):

...        # print sequence of numbers from 1 up till the given number

...        cnt = 1

...        while (cnt <= num):

...            print(cnt, end=", ")

...            cnt = cnt + 1 # can also write as cnt += 1

...
```

We have created a simple function using the "def" keyword. The function, named "prntseq" prints a sequence of numbers from one to the ending limit passed during the function call. The "num" function variable takes on the passing argument so we can use it in the function *definition*. Let's run the function with an argument of 10.

```
>>> prntseq(11)

1, 2, 3, 4, 5, 6, 7, 8, 9, 10, 11
```

We can also give an expression as an argument and Python will pass the result to the function. Here is a simple example.

```
>>> prntseq(5*3)
```

1, 2, 3, 4, 5, 6, 7, 8, 9, 10, 11, 12, 13, 14, 15

A function can take an unlimited number of arguments, but it's good practice to limit arguments of every function to a maximum of two. We should divide our function into smaller functions if there is a need to use more than two arguments. We created a multiplication generator script a couple of pages ago. Let's create a function to get the same output.

```
>>> def mlt_tbl(mul, timz):
...         print('Multiplication table of %d' % mul )
...         for seq in range(1,timz+1):
...         print("%d x %d = %d" % (mul, timz, mul*timz))
...
>>> mlt_tbl(9,12)
```

Multiplication table of 9

9 x 1 = 9

9 x 2 = 18

9 x 3 = 27

9 x 4 = 36

9 x 5 = 45

9 x 6 = 54

9 x 7 = 63

9 x 8 = 72

9 x 9 = 81

9 x 10 = 90

9 x 11 = 99

9 x 12 = 108

When there are hundreds of functions in your script there are few things to keep in mind.

1. Add exception handling whenever using arguments in expressions because the wrong data type can break execution
2. Create a function template and stick to it for all functions. This will help you have better expectations. A function definition should be divided into smaller chunks such as imports, variable assignments including all input(), actual work on the data, and in the end the return or other form of output such as print().
3. Use operators and methods that return the same output for all or most of the data types.

```
>>> def dosum(numx, numy):

...         print numx+numy

...

>>> dosum(7845, "this a string")

TypeError: unsupported operand type(s) for +: 'int' and 'str'
```

This shows how important it is to deploy exception handling and type conversion together when creating functions.

The Concept of Recursion

You can call a function inside its own definition creating a sort of loop to perform the same action consecutively on a data. It's like using a hammer to put up a nail on the wall. A lot of times, especially when dealing with numbers, we perform an operation that gives us a result and we have to perform the operation on that result again. Here's a simple example of recursion to find the factorial of an integer. Factorial of a number is the product of all numbers from one to that number. For example, the factorial of 4 is 1*2*3*4 = 24.

```
def get_fact(num):

        if x == 1:

                return 1
```

```
        else:

            return (num * get_fact(num - 1))
```

When we test the above function with "print(get_fact(6))", we get the output as 720, which is correct because 1*2*3*4*5*6 = 720. Note that we have declared a base condition, a condition that once met will stop the recursion. In the above code, "x == 1" is that base condition. We are using the knowledge that when a function is called from another function, the execution of the latter function is suspended until execution of the former function ends.

Variable Scope

In Python, variables have local scope by default. What does local scope mean? It means if you define a variable inside a function definition, it is not accessible in another function's definition. If we want a variable to be available in all function definitions, we can declare them outside of all function definitions. Another method is to use the "global" keyword.

```
x = 123 # this is a global variable


def tstFun():

    y = 789 # this is a global variable

    print(x + y)


tstFun()
```

Class and Objects

When we build something in real-life, we need a blueprint or schematic so we know what to put where. Classes are the blueprints of programming languages that are used to construct objects. They are the basis of object-oriented programming and help program complex concepts by replicating the same features multiple times.

```
>>> class frstcls:
```

```
...          prp = 554

...
```

Variable "prp" is known as a class property. We can create new objects once the class has been defined.

```
>>> obj1 = frstcls()

>>> obj1.prp

554
```

Every object created using the frstcls() class will inherit the property "prp". We can also create functions to the class that will become object methods. In fact, every class must have the __init__() function which is sort of an initiation function. The __init__() function is used to declare all properties of the class and optionally set their values, it can also be used to declare dependencies. Classes and objects are much more prevalent in video games where these concepts are used to create non-player characters to enrich the gaming experience. Most non-player characters share the same design and mechanics with cosmetic changes.

```
>>> class npc:

...          def __init__(instance,type,id,health,armor,mechanics):

...          instance.type = type

...          instance.id = id

...          instance.health = health

...          instance.armor = armor

...          instance.mechanics = mechanics

...
```

Every object created by the class is its "instance" which is what is passed to the __init__() function. Let's use our class to create an npc player.

```
>>> npc1 = npc("Mercenary", "Sailor", 75, 0, [2, 'walk', 'shoot'])
```

We can access individual object parameters easily like below.

```
>>> npc1.armor
```

25

>>> npc100 = npc("Level Boss","Pirate King",1000,500,[5, 'fast move', 'double 'jump', 'move tracker', 'slasher', 'unlit revolver'])

If you think that's a tough one, wait for the final level boss!

All object parameters are mutable unless we have an immutable data structure like a tuple.

>>> plyratk = 80

>>> if plyratk >= 75:

...   npc1.hp = 0

... else:

...   npc1.hp = npc1.hp - plyratk

...

>>> npc1.hp

0

We can perform all other methods that we have used for data structures and variables up till now, and then some on objects.

>>> del npc1.specialmoves

>>> del npc2

Scheduling and Automating Python Scripts

We can use the "Task Scheduler" that comes standard with all Windows installations to schedule and automate any tasks including execution of Python scripts.

Search "Task Scheduler" in Windows 10 start menu. An application with the same name will appear in the search results, select it. Currently, the application looks like the following screenshot.

A new window "Create Basic Task Wizard" will popup when "Create Basic Task" is clicked.

The step by step process is detailed below:

1. Enter a memorable and recognizable name so identifying different tasks later would become easier. It is also recommended to add a concise description. Click "Next".
2. We have to set a trigger which can be a specific time or an event in another Windows application or system. Whenever the trigger would occur, Windows will run the scheduled task. Select "Daily" for now.
3. Let us set 11:59pm "everyday" and whatever the current date is as the starting point. Keep one in the recur field because we are going for a daily schedule. Click "Next".
4. We want to run a Python script so we will keep the option "Start a program" selected. Click "Next".
5. In the final step, we have to direct Windows which program we want to schedule. To schedule a Python script, we should first run Python interpreter and then load the script as an argument. For example, if the Python interpreter is located at "C:\Python\python.exe" and the script you want to run is located at "D:\myscript.py".

Create Basic Task Wizard X

 Start a Program

Create a Basic Task

Trigger	**Program/script:**
Daily	C:\Python\python.exe Browse...
Action	
Start a Program	**Add arguments (optional):** D:\myscript.py
Finish	**Start in (optional):**

Click "Next" and you will see a summary of the task you have setup. Click on "Finish" to create the scheduled task you have setup that will run everyday at 11:59 pm.

It is such a good way to automate your daily tasks!

If you do not want to pass an argument or if the above process does not work for you, you can also schedule a Python script through the Windows Batch (.bat) file that are basically Windows script files. To schedule this way, we can add the following instruction to a batch file.

C:\Python\python.exe "D:\myscript.py"

Make sure to save the file. Now, we can schedule the batch file using the Windows "Task Scheduler" and Windows will execute the Python script.

This was a tutorial on how to create a very simple scheduled task. The "Task Scheduler" also offers many advanced options that are out of the scope of this book but you should explore them. There are a lot of similar tools available in Windows that an average user does not know about. It's always fun to explore new things!

Chapter 4: Basic Data Analysis

Everything in this world is constantly generating data. If we can record that data, we can process it to find the hidden meanings. It can help in making important decisions regarding your business or life. In this chapter, we will take a look at the basic data analysis concepts.

Data Parsing

There are many different ways to access data from the same file type. There are several libraries and depending upon the Python installation for the operating system in use (Windows in our case), there are even more options available.

Excel

MS Excel is the most widely used spreadsheet software in both personal and commercial domain. Due to this reason, there are several options to get data from MS Excel spreadsheets. In the below example, we are leveraging the Windows client for Python to get data from an excel sheet. Note that this Windows client method can be used to integrate with any application running on Windows operating system.

```python
import win32com.client as win32


exc=win32.gencache.EnsureDispatch('Excel.Application')

exc.Visible=True

filepath = "" # set the file path here

wrkbk = exc.Workbooks.Open(filepath)

wrksht = wrkbk.Worksheets('Sheet1') # get the sheet with the name "Sheet1"

wrksht.Name = 'Python Created' # change the name of that sheet

wrksht.Cells(1, 1).Value = "Hello" # set the value of the first cell in the worksheet
```

As you can notice, the first cell in the worksheet has row and column values of one.

An alternate approach

An alternative is to use another library specifically made to read data from an Excel file. We are going to use "xlrd" library.

wrkbk = xlrd.open_workbook(filepath)

One issue with "xlrd", which is not an issue but an inconvenience when you are developing a script, and actually an improvement from the user-side perspective, is that the Excel file is not visible so you have no idea what the Excel file looks like.

Once we have the workbook, we can access any sheet using its name or index.

wrksht = workbook.sheet_by_name('Sheet1') # access the sheet by the title of 'Sheet1'

wrksht = workbook.sheet_by_index(0) # access sheet with its position

In an Excel workbook, the position of a sheet can be changed so it's better to get sheets using their name and not the index.

print wrksht.cell(0, 0).value

In the "xlrd" library, the first cell of a sheet has a row and column indices of zero. To get all the values in a spreadsheet, we can use nested for loop to access each sheet and all the cells in it. One problem though, if we accidentally try to access a cell that is empty, we will get an error. For example, consider that the cell(100, 100) is empty. The following will result in an error.

print wrksht.cell(100, 100).value

To avoid this issue, we can read the number of rows and columns with data in an Excel sheet like below.

print("number of rows:", wrksht.nrows) # get number of rows with data

print("number of columns:", wrksht.ncols) # get number of columns with data

Using the above information, we can correctly set the limits on our "for" loops.

CSV

Comma Separated Values (CSV) files are a common method to distribute data over the internet due to its low file size. In data analysis, most of the times you will be reading and writing data in this format. They are essentially a text file where every data value is separated by a comma. For example, here is an example of some CSV data.

name,department,designation

Sinclair,IT,network engineer

Jones,Sales,inside salesperson

Sasha,HR,hiring manager

Alexa,Admin,VP secretary

The code to read the comma separated data from a CSV file saved in the same directory as the script file.

```
import csv

import os, sys


curdir=os.path.dirname(sys.argv[0]) # gets the directory where the script file is located

filep = os.path.join(curdir,"employee_data.csv")


with open(filep, mode='r') as csv_file:

        csv_read = csv.DictReader(csv_file)

        line_cnt = 0

        for row in csv_read:

                if line_cnt == 0:

                        print('Column names are',row.keys())

                        line_cnt += 1

                print(row['name'],"works in ",row['department'],"as a/an ",row['designation'])

                line_cnt += 1

                print('Processed',line_cnt,"lines")
```

This will output:

>>> Column names are ['name', 'department', 'designation']

Sinclair works in IT as a/an network engineer

Jones works in Sales as a/an inside salesperson

Sasha works in HR as a/an hiring manager

Alexa works in Admin as a/an VP secretary

Processed 5 lines

The first line of output that has the column names might not have the column names in this order because we are reading data by storing in a dictionary and we already know dictionaries are unordered data structures. When reading as a dictionary, the key is set as the first row header value of that column and the data from the relevant row. But, what would happen if there are no column headers? We might have to add a column header before we use this method.

To write a csv file, we can store all our data in a dictionary and that dictionary content is written to a csv formatted text file.

```
import csv

import os, sys


curdir=os.path.dirname(sys.argv[0])

filep = os.path.join(curdir,"join_date.csv")


with open(filep, mode='w') as csv_write:

        col_hdr = ['Name', 'Join Date', 'Salary']

        fin_file = csv.DictWriter(csv_write, fieldnames=col_hdr)


        fin_file.writeheader()

        fin_file.writerow({'Name': 'Sinclair', 'Join Date': '12-Mar-13', 'Salary':
'45,000'})
```

```
        fin_file.writerow({'Name': 'Jones', 'Join Date': '07-Jun-09', 'Salary':
'58,500'})

        fin_file.writerow({'Name': 'Sasha', 'Join Date': '07-Jun-09', 'Salary':
'85,000'})

        fin_file.writerow({'Name': 'Alexa', 'Join Date': '07-Jun-09', 'Salary':
'65,500'})
```

Websites

Everything you do online is recorded by someone with the chief purpose of knowing about you and marketing you relevant ads. It sounds cool but, personally, I think it pushes humans to become too much of a habitual animal. If you keep getting bombarded with things you like, not only its frustrating, it also affects your behaviour. For example, I like sushi but that doesn't mean wherever I go I only want to eat sushi! Where's the fun of exploring new food and places and experiencing the adventure of trying the unknown? I do not want everything I do recorded and analyzed. Or, if I do, I want to be compensated for it!

But, truth be told, there are various other applications of data recording and analysis besides shoving ads in your face. There have been huge strides in technology, especially in the fields of medicine and agriculture by knowing more about the environment and all the other factors involved. Precise predictions are regularly made about the weather which help the general public in planning different aspects of their daily lives.

The world wide web is a huge resource of free and paid data. You can tap into this resource to create applications to make lives better for the people. But, the rules of ethics should not be broken in any case. It's the weight of the world on the shoulders of data analysts and scientists - if you stumble upon information that is true but too dangerous, do you show it to the world or forward it to the global stakeholders? As Spiderman once said, power comes with responsibility!

Python has several libraries for web scraping as well. We are going to use "scrapy" now. Note that "scrapy" is usually used for large projects. For simpler web scraping projects, we can use libraries such as "BeautifulSoup".

Using Scrapy

You have to install the "scrapy" library before you use it.

pip install scrapy

After the installation is finished, we have to setup a project. This is done for every website we have to scrap. In the "scrapy" library, each scraper we build is called a spider, because spiders crawl. Using the Windows command prompt, navigate to the directory where we want to create the project and then run the following command.

scrapy startproject frstspydr

You do not have to name your crawler spider, especially if they give you the heebie jeebies! A new folder with the name "frstspydr" will be created in the directory that we navigated to.

The first step is to update the "\frstspydr\frstspydr\settings.py". In the "settings.py" file, two changes need to be made. We have to uncomment the "ITEMS_PIPELINE" tuple in case it's commented out and make edits so the file content looks as below.

#Export as CSV Feed

FEED_FORMAT = "csv"

FEED_URI = "reddit.csv"

The above lines indicate we are going to save the scraped information in a CSV formatted life. We are using a Reddit name because we are going to scrap a Reddit thread.

Going back to the command prompt, run the following command.

scrapy genspider redditcrawl www.reddit.com/r/breakingbad/

The above command will create a new spider inside the "\frstspydr\frstspydr\spiders\" folder using a standard template. We are going to use this newly created spider to get all the text and images from theBreaking Bad show Reddit thread.

If you open the "\frstspydr\frstspydr\spiders\redditcrawl.py" file, the below code is visible.

```
import scrapy


class RedditbotSpider(scrapy.Spider):

                name = 'redditcrawl'

                allowed_domains = ['www.reddit.com/r/breakingbad']

                start_urls = ['http://www.reddit.com/r/breakingbad']
```

```
def parse(self, response):

    pass
```

Some observations:

1. The spider can be named anything
2. The allowed_domains adds security by setting the domain that can be crawled using this crawler. This is entirely optional
3. Upon successful crawl, the parse function is called and executed

Next step is to update the start_urls argument in the RedditcrawlSpider class so it has the correct HTTPS format URL. Most websites nowadays have the secured HTTPS and we cannot access data from those sites using the unsecured URL version.

```
start_urls = ['https://www.reddit.com/r/breakingbad/']
```

See the "pass" inside the parse() function. Replace that with the following code block.

```
def parse(self, response):

        # Extract the html text with the css class selector

        title =
response.css('h3._eYtD2XCVieq6emjKBH3m::text').extract()

        images_url = response.css("img::attr(src)").extract()

        # Gather the data for every row

        for item in zip(titles,images_url):

                # store all the data in a dictionary

                scraped_info = {

                        'title' : item[0],

                        'images_url': item[1],

                }


        # Send all the scraped info to scrapy
```

```
    yield scraped_info
```

We have used the html class selector. We are going to use the css class values of html to get the text content (the post titles) and featured image URLs. Let's save the file and start using the crawler. The following command starts the crawler bot.

```
scrapy crawl redditcrawl
```

Before running the scrapper, make sure to change the working directory using the command prompt to the directory where the redditcrawl scraper resides. Not changing the directory and running the above command will result in an error.

While the crawler is running, it will output a lot of lines on the screen, but you can ignore all of them. After the crawl process is finished, you can navigate to the folder where you saved the crawler and find the reddit.csv file. The file will have all the post titles and direct URLs to the featured images, one in a row.

We can also download the images by creating a pipeline

```
ITEM_PIPELINES = {

  'scrapy.pipelines.images.ImagesPipeline': 1

}

IMAGES_STORE = '' # add the folder path where the images should be stored
```

If you are going to download the image files, make sure to comment out the CSV creation code we added earlier because sometimes performing both together leads to conflicts.

You can customize the crawler to get anything from any website. The "scrapy" framework supports multithreading which means you can deal with tons of online data without any compromise on performance. Still, be careful because this framework uses a lot of processing power. Smart programming goes a long way here.

Using BeautifulSoup

Beautiful Soup is a web scraping library in Python better suited for simpler tasks. It is way faster and easier to use to extract specific information from a website. First we install the library.

```
pip install BeautifulSoup4
```

Beautiful Soup extracts data from a website but is not able to make a connection with it. We need another library such as "urllib.request" to establish a secure connection with the website so Beautiful Soup can work.

We will scrape data from "example.webscraping.com" which has 25 pages containing the names and flags of all the countries in the world. The homepage URL is:

http://example.webscraping.com/

The URl of the last page is:

http://example.webscraping.com/places/default/index/25

This website is unsecured and the URLs share a common structure. Utilizing the inspection tool of Google Chrome, we inspect the html markup of the website. We notice that individual html elements do not have unique attributes, therefore we will extract accordingly by filtering through specific html elements.

The complete code is presented below along with comments for easier understanding.

```python
from bs4 import BeautifulSoup

import time

import urllib.request


webURL = "http://example.webscraping.com/"


for pag in range(0, 26): # 0-26 because we have 25 pages where second page is '1'

    if pag == 0:

        lnk = webURL

    else:

        lnk = webURL + "places/default/index/" + str(pag)

    try:

        time.sleep(1)

'''
```

Beautiful Soup reads data very quickly, too quickly for most servers' liking. If they see your script sending several requests to the site very quickly, they will think you are trying to hack or DDoS the site. To prevent that from happening, the server can temporarily block your IP. We are adding a delay of 1 second between consecutive server requests so that situation never happens.

```
    '''

                page = urllib.request.urlopen(lnk)

            soup = BeautifulSoup(page, 'html.parser')

                cntry_names = soup.find_all('td') # get all country names in a
page

                cntry_flags = soup.find_all('img') #get all flag's image URL in a
page

        except:

                print("Something bad happened while trying to scrap the
website.")

        if (cntry_names): # only run the following 'for' loop if content_id is not
empty

            for  name in cntry_names:

                    print(name.text.lstrip()) #lstrip() removes any
unwanted spaces from the text

        if (cntry_flags): # only run the following 'for' loop if content_img is not
empty

            for itr in cntry_flags:

                    print(webURL + itr['src'].lstrip('/')) #lstrip() removes
extra forward slashes from the URL
```

The above code opens each website page and gets the country name and the country flag. We can also store this gathered data in a CSV file so we can access it later without having to scrap the website another time.

```
f = open('scrapData.csv','w')

if (content_td): # only run the following 'for' loop if content_id is not empty

                for itm in content_td:
```

```
            f.write(itm.text.lstrip())
```

```
if (content_img): # only run the following 'for' loop if content_img is not empty
```

```
        for itr in content_img:
```

```
            f.write(webURL + itr['src'].lstrip('/'))
```

Working with NumPy

The "numpy" library provides us with one more data structure: the numpy arrays. These arrays closely resemble the mathematical matrices. In fact, all the matrix concepts can be applied on the numpy arrays. We have to install the array before using it.

```
pip install numpy
```

Once installed, we can start using the library.

```
import numpy as np
```

```
arr = np.array([36, 69])
```

```
brr = np.array([[75, 53],
```

```
                [95, 51]])
```

```
print(arr.ndim) #get dimension of array which is returns the number of rows in the array
```

The number of elements in each row must be the same in a multidimensional array. The output of the above script is:

```
1
```

To get the number of rows and columns, we have to use the "shape" property.

```
print(arr.shape) # for a multidimensional array, returns a tuple containing number of rows then number of columns, for a single dimensional array, the number of columns is returned
```

```
print(brr.shape)
```

The output is:

```
(2,)
```

```
(2, 2)
```

The numpy arrays look very similar to nested lists, but support many methods that we cannot apply on nested lists. To see how many items are in an array, we use the "size" property.

```
print(brr.size) # returns 6 because total 6 elements are present in the "brr" array
```

Individual elements in the array can be accessed using the indices just like in a list, but the syntax is a little different. In a numpy array, the first row - first column position has 0, 0 index.

```
print(arr[1,1]) #outputs 53 because 1, 1 means second row and second column
```

As the name suggests, *num*py arrays are geared towards number types. But, we can also store strings with the requirement that all elements in an array must be of same data type.

```
crr = np.array([111, "is called", " a Nelson", True])
```

```
print(crr)
```

The output will be.

```
['111' 'is called' ' a Nelson' 'True']
```

The numpy library converted all the data to the string type. We have to be careful because during data analysis, if we program our script to find the boolean "True" value in this array, the script will always return null because the boolean "True" has been converted to the string "True". Another observation is that the commas are missing but that's just what printing a numpy array looks like. We can print another array just to be sure.

```
print(bArr)
```

```
[[75 53]
```

```
 [95 51]]
```

What if we have an array that has only numbers and Boolean values? Here is an example:

```
drr = np.array([183, True, False])
```

```
print(drr)
```

The output is:

```
[183  1  0]
```

The numbers one and zero are numerical equivalents of Boolean "True" and "False".

Numpy arrays cannot be changed once created. Although, new arrays can be made by manipulating the existing array.

```
err = np.append(arr, 3347)
```

```
print(err)
```

The output is:

```
[ 36          69          3347]
```

Reminder: leading zeros are not allowed in Python numbers anymore.

```
frr = np.array([14.7, 3.00])
```

```
print(frr)
```

Which gives us the output of:

```
[14.7 3. ]
```

Appending data in a multidimensional array creates a new one-dimensional array.

```
grr = np.append(brr[0], 4) #new one dimensional array
```

```
print(grr)
```

The output is:

```
[ 75 53 95 51  4]
```

Removing an element from an array also leads to creation of a new array.

```
hrr = np.delete(grr, 3) #this method removes an element by finding it through its index. 3 has index of 4 in grr
```

```
print(hrr)
```

The output is:

```
[75 53 95 51]
```

There are many standard arrays that are used in various applications. The numpy library has special methods to create such arrays quickly.

```
zrr = np.zeros((2, 3)) #this will create an array with all elements zero in floating type

print(zrr)
```

```
zrrint = np.zeros((2, 3), dtype=int) # if we want to create an array of integer zeros

print(zrrint)
```

The outputs are.

```
[[0. 0. 0.]

 [0. 0. 0.]]

[[0 0 0]

 [0 0 0]]
```

We can also create a three-dimensional (3D) array.

```
threDrr = np.ones((2, 3, 3)) #this is taken as a multidimensional (3D) array consisting of two 2D arrays each of 3 rows and 3 columns

print(threDrr)
```

The output is:

```
[[[1. 1. 1.]

  [1. 1. 1.]

  [1. 1. 1.]]
```

[[1. 1. 1.]

[1. 1. 1.]

[1. 1. 1.]]]

If you want the elements of an array to follow a specific sequence, we can do that with a couple of methods.

seqrr = np.arange(0, 101, 10) #create an array with elements in a sequence by setting how much interval should be added between each element

print(seqrr)

linrr = np.linspace(0, 100, 11, dtype=int) #create an array with elements in a sequence by setting how many elements are needed in the array. Python automatically sets the appropriate step value

print(linArr)

The outputs is:

[0 10 20 30 40 50 60 70 80 90 100]

[0 10 20 30 40 50 60 70 80 90 100]

A few things to remember:

1.   linspace() includes the maximum value in the sequence unlike the arange() which works like the range()
2.   linspace() creates sequence in floating type numbers unless instructed otherwise just like in our example ("dtype=int").

To create an array with all element positions taken by the same number, we use the full() method.

fillrr = np.full((2,2), 7)

print(fillrr)

The code outputs the following:

[[7 7]

 [7 7]]

As stated earlier, the numpy arrays are the closest implementation of matrices in Python. As such, there are various methods available in numpy library to perform matrix operations. Identity matrix are used frequently in matrix operations and we can create an identity matrix as a numpy array with a single line of code.

idrr = np.eye(2, dtype=int) #identity matrix always has the same number of rows and columns (i.e they are square matrices) and one of the diagonals has all elements set as '1'

print(idrr)

The output is:

[[1 0]

 [0 1]]

The numpy library has randomizer methods that generate random integer or float numbers to fill in an array. This is particularly useful when you want to create several arrays to test a script.

randIrr = np.random.randint(1, 15, size=(4, 4)) #1 and 15 are minimum and maximum limits so numpy will generate random numbers that lie within this range. (4, 4) will be the size of new array created

print(randIrr)

randFrr = np.random.random((3, 3)) #this time we didn't give any limits and the returned array will have a size of 3 rows and 3 columns

print(randFrr)

The output of the above code is below. You will see different output when you run the code because randomizer will output different numbers.

[[7 8 9 9]

 [5 14 7 2]

 [3 2 9 13]

 [1 3 8 8]]

[[0.29457456 0.83468151 0.35160973]

[0.29059067 0.896374607 0.38657756]

[0.5831767 0.54060431 0.94441115]]

Below are some examples of operations you can perform on numpy arrays.

arr = np.array([

[7, 8, 9],

[9, 8, 7]

])

brr = np.array([

[1, 2, 3],

[3, 2, 1]

])

#addition

print(np.add(arr, brr)) # this is a scalar addition which we can also do with '+' operator like arr + brr

#subtraction

print(np.subtract(arr, brr)) #again a scalar operation hence aArr - bArr also gives same output

#multiplication

print(np.multiply(arr, brr)) # element by element (scalar) which is also arr * brr

#division

```
print(np.divide(arr, brr)) #also aArr / bArr because a scalar operation
```

The output of the above script is:

```
[[ 8 10 12]

 [12 10 8]]

[[6 6 6]

 [6 6 6]]

[[ 7 16 27]

 [27 16 7]]

[[7. 4.      3.]

 [3. 4.      7.]]
```

We can also perform dot and cross products on arrays.

```
drr = np.array([

        [7, 8, 9],

        [9, 8, 7],

        [4, 5, 6]

])

err = np.array([

        [1, 2, 3],

        [3, 2, 1],

        [4, 5, 6]

])

#dot product

print(np.dot(drr, err))
```

#cross product

print(np.cross(drr, err))

The outputs are:

[[67 75 83]

[61 69 77]

[43 48 53]]

[[6 -12 6]

[-6 12 -6]

[0 0 0]]

Dot and cross products play a significant role in vector theory. You can read about it online. To transpose an array, we have the property 'T'.

print(drr.T)

The output is:

[[7 9 4]

[8 8 5]

[9 7 6]]

Finding different kind of sums results in many interesting values.

print(np.sum(drr)) #sum all elements in an array, returns a single value

#sum the elements in either the rows or columns

print(np.sum(drr, axis=0)) # axis = 0 means we sum all elements in the rows

print(np.sum(drr, axis=1)) # axis = 1 means we sum all elements in the columns

Here are the outputs:

63

[20 21 22]

[24 24 15]

Chapter 5: Advanced Data Analysis

Chapter 4 has a lot of information on data analysis, but Python supports much more advanced data analysis tools.

Using pandas Framework

When it comes to data analysis, Python has another ace up its sleeve: the "pandas" framework. The framework provides two new data structures, "series" and "dataframe". The framework also provides out of the box data acquisition techniques for all popular data sources such as spreadsheets and CSV files. Without wasting another minute, let us dive into the concepts and working of this library.

pandas Series

The "pandas" Series data structure has features combined from both dictionaries and numpy arrays. It is an advanced way of declaring and manipulating a group of numbers with a specific sequence.

```
from pandas import Series

import pandas as pd



asr = Series([1, 7, 9]) # the syntax closely resembles that of a numpy array



print(asr)

print(asr.values)  # get all values as a list just like a dictionary

print(asr.index)  # get all indices as a list, we can say they are the "keys" of this data structure - another resemblance with a dictionary. Since we didn't set specific keys, the values were assigned number indices



kes = ['1st', '2nd', '3rd']

bsr = Series([3, 9, 7], index=kes) # we can set custom "keys" for the data structure
```

```python
print(bsr)

print(bsr[1st'])  # get element using key just like a dictionary

print(bsr[0])  # get element using index just like any other data structure in Python


adic = {

        '1st': 245,

        '2nd': 265,

        '3rd': 888

}

csr = Series(adic)  # creating a series from a dictionary is very easy


print(csr)


ind = ['1st', '2nd', '4th']

dsr = Series(adic, index=ind)  # if a key isn't in the original dictionary (4th isn't present
in this case), "NaN" is added as value for that key


print(dsr)


print(pd.isnull(dsr['4th']))  # check if an element has "NaN" value, in this case the
output will be Boolean True


dsr.name = 'Info' # give name to entire series

dSer.index.name = 'Key' # give name to the index/key column
```

```
print(dsr)
```

```
dsr.index = ['un', 'deux', 'nul']  # we can change the keys of a series, this is a major
upgrade from a dictionary where the keys are immutable. Changing the indices/keys
removes any name we have given to the index column
```

```
print(dsr)
```

The outputs of the above "print" statements are.

```
0          1

1          7

2          9

dtype: int64

[1 7 9]

RangeIndex(start=0, stop=3, step=1)

1st        3

2nd        9

3rd        7

dtype: int64

3

3

1st        245

2nd        265

3rd        888
```

dtype: int64

1st   245.0

2nd   265.0

4th   NaN

dtype: float64

True

Key

1st   245.0

2nd   265.0

4th   NaN

Name: Info, dtype: float64

un   245.0

deux   265.0

nul   NaN

Name: Info, dtype: float64

Time series

A quantity that can be measured with respect to time can be represented as a time series - a special type of pandas Series where the index column has time values. If you take a look at any log file, you will notice how each entry is preceded by a timestamp showing when that particular log entry was made. The logs are sorted according to time, either latest to earliest or vice versa.

The pandas framework provides a lot of methods to manipulate time series that are beneficial in various applications. All the rules of pandas series work on time series but we need to understand how Python works with dates before we can move on to the next topic. The below script shows different manipulation techniques of time.

from datetime import datetime

from datetime import timedelta

```python
from dateutil.parser import parse


nowTime = datetime.now()  # get the current date and time value


print(now)  # the returned data has the current date and time including the year,
month, day, hour, minutes, seconds, milliseconds, and microseconds values


nxT = nowTime + timedelta(12)  # timedelta() creates time object that can be used to
jump time according to the arguments provided. In this case, we want to get the date
and time 12 days from current date and time


print(nxT)


print(str(nxT))  # string looks the same as datatime format


print(nxT.strftime('%Y-%m-%d'))  # reformat datetime value


impTime = '2016-11-09'


print(datetime.strptime(impTime, '%Y-%m-%d'))  # format string as datetime


print(parse(impTime))  # when the string has a format that's the same as a datetime
format, we don't need to use strptime() and declare a format. We can use parse() to
quickly convert such string to a datetime object


print(parse(ranTime, dayfirst=True))  # the dayfirst argument swaps the position of
months with days to follow the international date and time convention.
```

The respective outputs of the above print statements are:

2019-10-30 08:10:25.841218

2019-11-11 08:10:25.841218

2019-11-11 08:10:25.841218

2019-11-11

2016-11-09 00:00:00

2016-11-09 00:00:00

2016-09-11 00:00:00

pandas DataFrames

The dataframe is the most advanced data structure in Python and can handle gigabytes of data processing without slowing down the computer. Thanks to the process optimizations done behind the scenes, pandas dataframes are ideal for all data analysis and machine learning applications.

Let us take a look at some basic dataframe manipulation.

```
import pandas as pd


monLst = ['Jan', 'Feb', 'Mar', 'Apr']


quartrStats = {

        "Ad Spending": [12000, 24000, 9000, 11000],

        "Revenue": [55000, 15745, 21000, 47314],

        "Store Manager": ['Jones', 'Joshua', 'Marcus', 'Smith']

}
```

```
dfnew = pd.DataFrame(quartrStats, index=monLst)  # assigning custom keys/indices
to the dataframe
```

```
dfalt = pd.DataFrame(quartrStats)  # creating a dataframe with default keys/indices
```

```
dfalt.set_index('Store Manager', inplace=True)  # assign an existing data column as
the index column, "inplace" argument makes sure the original dataframe is
overwritten with the change. By default, whenever a change is made to a dataframe,
the original is kept intact and a new dataframe is created to carry the changes.
```

```
print(dfnew)
```

```
print(dfalt)
```

The output is:

	Ad Spending	Revenue	Store Manager
Jan	12000	55000	Jones
Feb	24000	15745	Joshua
Mar	9000	21000	Marcus
Apr	11000	47314	Smith

	Ad Spending	Revenue
Store Manager		
Jones	12000	55000
Joshua	24000	15745
Marcus	9000	21000
Smith	11000	47314

We can extract a single column or a set of columns from a dataframe. Converting a dataframe column to a numpy array is also straightforward, which leads to the million dollar question: can we use a numpy array to create a dataframe? The code below actually performs all these tasks.

```
print(dfnew['Revenue'])  # a new series is created with the same index as the source
dataframe
```

print(dfnew.Revenue) # this will only work if the column header has no spaces, therefore it is a good idea to use underscores '_' or dashes '-' instead of spaces when adding column header in a dataframe

print(dfnew[['Ad Spending', 'Revenue']]) # use multiple columns of a dataframe to create a new dataframe with the same index as the original one

print(np.array(dfnew[['Ad Spending', 'Revenue']])) # convert the newly extracted dataframe to a numpy array

The output of the above script is:

Jan   55000

Feb   15745

Mar   21000

Apr   47314

Name: Revenue, dtype: int64

Jan   55000

Feb   15745

Mar   21000

Apr   47314

Name: Revenue, dtype: int64

	Ad Spending	Revenue
Jan	12000	55000
Feb	24000	15745
Mar	9000	21000
Apr	11000	47314

```
[[12000          55000]

 [24000   15745]

 [9000    21000]

 [11000   47314]]
```

Parsing Data

"pandas" framework supports easy and fast data retrieval from various resources without the need of another library. Search the Internet for "AAPL", which is the stock price data of the global tech giant Apple Inc.. You can use a data aggregator service like Quandl. Let's download the data to the Python folder in the "csv" format. The following code will read all the downloaded data.

```python
import pandas as pd


# read local CSV data

datF = pd.read_csv('EOD-AAPL.csv') # this is the downloaded CSV file, replace it with the name of your file


datF.set_index('Date', inplace=True) # making date column the index of the dataframe

datF.to_csv("newF.csv")  # create a new CSV file and transfer all the dataframe data


print(datF.head()) # print the first five rows of the dataframe


datF = pd.read_csv('newF.csv', index_col=0)  # this is how to set a specific data column as an index column during data read using the column index. Zero index means the first column


print(datF.head())
```

```
datF.rename(columns={'Open': 'Open_Price'}, inplace=True) # we can rename a
single or multiple columns by passing the values as key-value pairs of a dictionary to
the rename() method


print(datF.head())


datF.to_csv("newFn.csv", header=False) # save data to a CSV file while ignoring the
column header


datF = pd.read_csv('newFn.csv', names=['Date', 'Open', 'High', 'Low', 'Close',
'Volume', 'Dividend', 'Split', 'Adj_Open', 'Adj_High', 'Adj_Low', 'Adj_Close',
'Adj_Volume'], index_col=0) # we can also set the column names when reading data
from a CSV file

print(datF.head())
```

The output of the above script is:

```
            Open     High      Low  ...    Adj_Low  Adj_Close  Adj_Volume

Date                                ...

2017-12-28 171.00  171.850  170.480 ... 165.957609 166.541693 16480187.0

2017-12-27 170.10  170.780  169.710 ... 165.208036 166.074426 21498213.0

2017-12-26 170.80  171.470  169.679 ... 165.177858 166.045222 33185536.0

2017-12-22 174.68  175.424  174.500 ... 169.870969 170.367440 16349444.0

2017-12-21 174.17  176.020  174.100 ... 169.481580 170.367440 20949896.0


[5 rows x 12 columns]

            Open High      Low  ...    Adj_Low  Adj_Close  Adj_Volume

Date                            ...

2017-12-28 171.00  171.850  170.480 ... 165.957609 166.541693 16480187.0
```

```
2017-12-27  170.10  170.780  169.710  ...  165.208036  166.074426  21498213.0

2017-12-26  170.80  171.470  169.679  ...  165.177858  166.045222  33185536.0

2017-12-22  174.68  175.424  174.500  ...  169.870969  170.367440  16349444.0

2017-12-21  174.17  176.020  174.100  ...  169.481580  170.367440  20949896.0


[5 rows x 12 columns]

                  Open_Price  High     Low  ...   Adj_Low  Adj_Close
Adj_Volume

Date                              ...

2017-12-28   171.00  171.850  170.480  ...  165.957609  166.541693  16480187.0

2017-12-27   170.10  170.780  169.710  ...  165.208036  166.074426  21498213.0

2017-12-26   170.80  171.470  169.679  ...  165.177858  166.045222  33185536.0

2017-12-22   174.68  175.424  174.500  ...  169.870969  170.367440  16349444.0

2017-12-21   174.17  176.020  174.100  ...  169.481580  170.367440  20949896.0


[5 rows x 12 columns]

                  Open  High     Low  ...   Adj_Low  Adj_Close  Adj_Volume

Date                              ...

2017-12-28  171.00  171.850  170.480  ...  165.957609  166.541693  16480187.0

2017-12-27  170.10  170.780  169.710  ...  165.208036  166.074426  21498213.0

2017-12-26  170.80  171.470  169.679  ...  165.177858  166.045222  33185536.0

2017-12-22  174.68  175.424  174.500  ...  169.870969  170.367440  16349444.0

2017-12-21  174.17  176.020  174.100  ...  169.481580  170.367440  20949896.0
```

[5 rows x 12 columns]

Write data

We can use pandas framework to write data in various common formats. Let's look at an example where we write data to an HTML file.

```
datF.to_html('datF.html')  # such as simple implementation
```

You can view this new HTML file by opening it up in any browser. To view the markup of this page, you can open it using any text editor. You can also use the inspection tool of the browser to view the markup.

Internet Scraping using pandas

We can scrape websites using the pandas special library "pandas_datareader". We need to install it using pip before we can use it.

```
pip install pandas_datareader
```

Run the following script after the installation has completed.

```
import pandas_datareader.data as web


rngstrt = '1/1/2009'

rngstp = '5/5/2015'


dfnew = web.get_data_yahoo('GOOG', rngstrt, rngstp)


print(dfnew.head()) #output first five rows of the dataframe
```

The output will be:

```
            High          Low ...    Volume  Adj Close
Date                  ...
2009-01-02  160.309128  152.179596 ...  7248000.0  160.060059
```

```
2009-01-05  165.001541  156.911850  ...  9814500.0  163.412491

2009-01-06  169.763687  162.585587  ...  12898500.0  166.406265

2009-01-07  164.837143  158.779861  ...  9022600.0  160.403763

2009-01-08  161.987823  158.077484  ...  7228300.0  161.987823
```

[5 rows x 6 columns]

Visualize Data

It is very difficult to even read thousands of lines of data, let alone find a relationship in the data. But, this becomes easier when we plot charts using the data. Many trends and system behaviours becomes instantly recognizable.

Plot a Chart

There are several libraries to create graphs using Python. We have already seen matplotlib in action. Let's work with pygal now. We can install this library using pip.

```
pip install pygal
```

All the codes in this section are inspired from the Pygal official documentation available at http://www.pygal.org/en/stable/documentation/. Here's a simple line chart generating code.

```python
import pygal

from pygal.style import LightenStyle

dark_lighten_style = LightenStyle('#000000')

bar_chart = pygal.Bar(style=dark_lighten_style)

bar_chart.add('Fibonacci', [0, 1, 1, 2, 3, 5, 8, 13, 21, 34, 55])

bar_chart.add('Padovan', [1, 1, 1, 2, 2, 3, 4, 5, 7, 9, 12])

bar_chart.render() # show the chart
```

```
bar_chart.render_to_file('bar_chart.svg') # save the chart as svg image file
```

Here is the output chart:

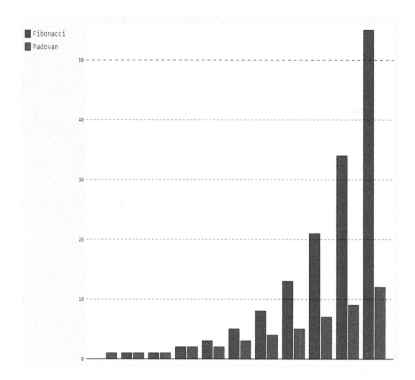

We are using the LightenStyle() to create a grayscale color scheme with the base color of black (hex code: #000000). We pass that custom color scheme as the style to be used for the chart. Pygal smartly chooses the best grayscale shades to plot the chart.

Let's create a pie chart.

```
import pygal

from pygal.style import LightenStyle


dark_lighten_style = LightenStyle('#000000')
```

```
pie_chart = pygal.Pie(style=dark_lighten_style)

pie_chart.title = 'Browser usage in February 2012 (in %)'

pie_chart.add('IE', 19.5)

pie_chart.add('Firefox', 36.6)

pie_chart.add('Chrome', 36.3)

pie_chart.add('Safari', 4.5)

pie_chart.add('Opera', 2.3)

pie_chart.render() # show the pie chart

pie_chart.render_to_file('pie_chart.svg') # save the chart as svg image file
```

The output chart looks like the following:

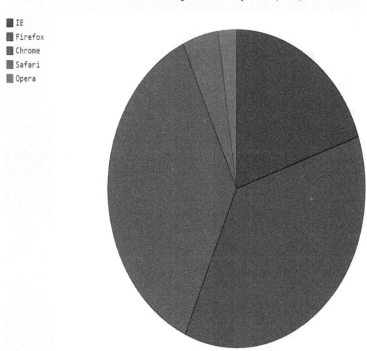

Notice how the Pygal is taking care of styling the chart legend and title. If we had used "matplotlib", we would have had to set all these things ourselves.

There are so many options available with Pygal and you should explore the library further. One last example we are going to cover is to create a box chart, which is a very common sight in financial applications, especially trading. Here's the complete code.

```python
import pygal

from pygal.style import LightenStyle


dark_lighten_style = LightenStyle('#000000')


box_plot = pygal.Box(style=dark_lighten_style)

box_plot.title = 'V8 benchmark results'

box_plot.add('Chrome', [6395, 8212, 7520, 7218, 12464, 1660, 2123, 8607])

box_plot.add('Firefox', [7473, 8099, 11700, 2651, 6361, 1044, 3797, 9450])

box_plot.add('Opera', [3472, 2933, 4203, 5229, 5810, 1828, 9013, 4669])

box_plot.add('IE', [43, 41, 59, 79, 144, 136, 34, 102])

box_plot.render_to_file('box_chart.svg') # save the chart as svg image file
```

The output:

Final note: "svg" format is still a relatively new format and you might not be able to open images with this format on your Windows computer. You can use your Google Chrome browser to view "svg" images.

Chapter 6: Web Applications with Python

Django is an external library widely used to create web applications using Python. It's used by online giants like Instagram and Pinterest. The codes in this chapter are inspired by the work of YouTube channel "techwithtim".

Setup Django

Let's install using pip.

pip install django

Now, let's create our first application. We need to setup the initiation files as a project that will serve as the environment of the application. Using the command prompt, navigate to a folder that will house the application files. To setup the application project, run the following command.

django-admin startproject firstapp

"firstapp" is the name of our first project. To see if the project is setup correctly, run the following command on the command prompt. Make sure you have changed current directory to the correct folder.

python manage.py runserver

To create an application inside this project environment, run the following command.

python manage.py startapp firstapp

Note that the project name and application can be different. To change the different application pages (called views), move to the application folder and change the file named "views.py".

views.py file

from django.http import HttpResponse

def index(request):

    return HttpResponse("This is a brand new web app!")

We need to create a URL to access this view. Let's create a new Python file "urls.py" in the application directory. Add the following code to it:

```
# urls.py

from django.urls import path


from . import views


urlpatterns = [

    path('', views.index, name='index'),

]
```

There is another "urls.py" if you navigate inside the application directory. Modify it so it has the following code.

```
# urls.py

from django.contrib import admin

from django.urls import include, path


urlpatterns = [

    path('', include(firstapp.urls')), # firstapp is the name of our app

    path('admin/', admin.site.urls),

]
```

You can view this web application by going to the following URL in the browser.

127.0.0.1:8000

First Web Application

Every web application that deals with data usually has a database to store information. We are going to set up an SQLite3 database for our application.

Go to the "settings.py" file inside the web application folder and add one line in the section.

\# Application definition

INSTALLED_APPS = [

  'django.contrib.admin',

  'django.contrib.auth',

  'django.contrib.contenttypes',

  'django.contrib.sessions',

  'django.contrib.messages',

  'django.contrib.staticfiles',

  'firstapp.apps.FirstappConfig', # <- add this line, firstapp is the name of our application

]

Now using command prompt, let's move to the directory containing "manage.py" and run the following command.

python manage.py migrate

This command will create an empty database in the application directory. We can add information in the database when needed.

Let's create an admin page. We will first need to setup the database correctly. Run the following command but first make sure you are in the directory that contains "manage.py"

python manage.py createsuperuser

You will now see an admin dashboard created. To view this newly created admin page, go to the following link

127.0.0.1:8000/admin

The admin dashboard is usually created to view the details of the web application. Let's put the database details in the dashboard by adding following block of code in the "admin.py".

```
from django.contrib import admin

from .models import ToDoList, Item

# Register your models here.

admin.site.register(ToDoList)

admin.site.register(Item)
```

Let's get a little fancy and start with HTML templates. Templates are a well-known concept in web designing nowadays. Templates are HTML files that can be shared by different pages that should have the same design and content. Of course, you can overwrite specific details of a template to show different stuff on a specific page. For this project, we are going to create a base HTML template file and then create two more HTML files that share that template. In the main folder, create a base.html and add the following code to it.

```
<html>

<head>

  <title>{% block title %}Tim's Site{% endblock %}</title>

</head>


<body>

  <div id="content" name="content">

                              {% block content %}

                              {% endblock %}

  </div>


</body>
```

```
</html>
```

Notice the places where we have used placeholders wrapped in "{% %}". We must include the closing "{% endblock %}" placeholder. We will insert custom content here when we create specific HTML files. Let's create home.html with the following code. The first line tells Python what parent template to use for this HTML file.

```
{% extends 'main/base.html' %}
```

```
{% block title %}
```

```
Home
```

```
{% endblock %}
```

```
{% block content %}
```

```
<h1>Home Page</h1>
```

```
{% endblock %}
```

Let's create the other HTML file that will use some Python conditional statements to generate the code. Variable names are enclosed in double spaces "{{}}".

```
{% extends "main/base.html" %}
```

```
{% block title %}View List{% endblock %}
```

```
{% block content %}
```

```
                                        <h1>{{ls.name}}</h1>
```

```
                                        <ul>
```

```
                                            {% for item in ls.item_set.all %}
```

```
                                                {% if item.complete == True
%}
```

```
                                                    <li>{{item.text}} -
COMPLETE</li>
```

```
                                        {% else %}

                                            <li>{{item.text}} -
INCOMPLETE</li>

                                        {% endif %}

                                {% endfor %}

                        </ul>

{% endblock %}
```

We have to update the "views.py" and "url.py" to start showing the new HTML files (pages) on the web application.

```python
# views.py

from django.shortcuts import render

from django.http import HttpResponse

from .models import ToDoList, Item

# Create your views here.


def index(response, id):

                        ls = ToDoList.objects.get(id=id)

                        return render(response, "main/list.html",
{"ls":ls})


def home(response):

                        return render(response,
"main/home.html", {})
```

The empty {} is used to pass a dictionary containing the variables to the templates.

```python
# urls.py
```

```python
from django.urls import path

from . import views

urlpatterns = [

path("<int:id>", views.index, name="index"),

path("", views.home, name="home")

]
```

After adding simple HTML page, let's add a simple HTML form. Let's create another template "formCreate.html" with the following code.

```html
{% extends 'main/base.html' %}

{% block title %}

Create New List

{% endblock %}


{% block content %}

                                            <h3>Create a New To Do List</h3>

                                            <br>

                                            <form method="post" action="/create/"
class="form-group">

                                                {% csrf_token %}

                                                <div class="input-group mb-3">

                                                        <div class="input-
group-prepend">

                                                                <button
```

name="save" type="submit" class="btn btn-success">Create</button>

</div>

{{form.name}}

</div>

</form>

{% endblock %}

We must use "{% csrf_token %}" in every form we create because it adds necessary security measures to the form. The {{form}} is set when creating a form using this template, you can say it will be the ID of that form.

Let's update "views.py" for this form.

def create(response):

   return render(response, "main/formCreate.html", {"form": form}) # goes inside views.py

We also have to update the "urls.py".

from django.urls import path

from . import views

urlpatterns = [

path("", views.home, name="home"),

path("home/", views.home, name="home"),

path("create/", views.create, name="index"),

path("<int:id>", views.index, name="index"),

]

We have to add the following code block to "views.py" to create a form instance using the formCreate.html

...

```
from .forms import CreateNewList

...

def create(request):

    form = CreateNewList()

    return render(request, "main/formCreate.html", {"form": form})
```

Now, we have built the form but there's no way to retrieve information from the form. Let's understand some HTML concepts.

POST Request: When information needs to be passed from the front-end (website interface) to the backend (server/database), POST HTML request is used. This is a secured and encrypted request.

GET Request: When information needs to be passed from the backend (server/database) to the front-end (website interface), POST HTML request is used. This is an open and unsecured request.

We have to add the POST and GET requests to the "views.py".

```
def create(response):

    if response.method == "POST":

        form = CreateNewList(response.POST)


        if form.is_valid():

            n = form.cleaned_data["name"]

            t = ToDoList(name=n)

            t.save()


        return HttpResponseRedirect("/%i" %t.id)
```

```
else:

    form = CreateNewList()



return render(response, "main/formCreate.html", {"form":form})
```

We can add Bootstrap stylizing and JavaScript customization to the django web application. What's Bootstrap? It's a style library available for free to make web applications responsive. To add these features, we have the change the base.html file. Replace <home> with <!doctype html> and add the following lines between <head> and </head>.

```
<meta charset="utf-8">
```

```
<meta name="viewport" content="width=device-width, initial-scale=1, shrink-to-fit=no">
```

```
<link rel="stylesheet" href="https://stackpath.bootstrapcdn.com/bootstrap/4.3.1/css/bootstrap.min.css">
```

Let's add the following codes just before the </body> tag.

```
<script src="https://code.jquery.com/jquery-3.3.1.slim.min.js"></script>
```

```
<script src="https://cdnjs.cloudflare.com/ajax/libs/popper.js/1.14.7/umd/popper.min.js"></script>
```

```
<script src="https://stackpath.bootstrapcdn.com/bootstrap/4.3.1/js/bootstrap.min.js"></script>
```

Now, we can add Bootstrap classes to the elements to make them better looking without writing our own stylesheet. We can also write JavaScript and jQuery codes for added dynamics.

The possibilities are endless with Django Python framework and there are even more Django extension libraries available. For example, to add the capability of user sign up we can use "django-crispy-forms" external library.

Chapter 7: GUI and Computer Peripheral Control

Working with command prompt might look nerdy cool at first, but it's not a good way to take inputs from users in today's world. Everything requires a visual touch. Python provides considerable resources and tools to create a Graphical User Interface (GUI). Let's create some fun things.

Create GUI for File and Folder Selection

We can give users the ability to visually navigate to a file and folder for various file operations. This is enabled by using Python's standard GUI library, Tkinter, a unique name with powerful GUI capabilities. The code enables a user to select a file so we can extract the file path.

```
import Tkinter

import tkFileDialog


rut = Tkinter.Tk()

rut.withdraw() #hide the tkinter window

fileAcc = tkFileDialog.askopenfile(parent=root,initialdir="/",mode='rb',title='Pick any file')

if fileAcc != None:

                            print fileAcc.name
```

We can restrict the file type the user can select through the GUI. Let's pass more arguments to the askopenfile() method.

```
fileAcc = tkFileDialog.askopenfile(parent=root,initialdir="/",mode='rb',title='Pick any file',filetypes = (("All Excel files","*.xl*"),("All files","*.*")))
```

Taking Control of Keyboard and Mouse

We are entering the domain of programming that can be attributed to hacking. Taking control of a keyboard and mouse can be used for nefarious purposes. But, there are benefits to teaching this topic.

1. Clients want to test their web applications. You can write a Python program to automatically test their web app in several ways. One script can do the work of an entire QA team.
2. You want to automate some tasks on your computer that will take too much time to directly integrate with Python. For example, instead of using an Excel related library to open an Excel spreadsheet, you can use this technique to achieve the same results.

The external library "pyautogui" helps us in this respect. No other library is required for a Windows system.

```
pip install pyautogui
```

When "pyautogui" takes control of either keyboard or mouse, it blocks your access to those devices. If you make an error in the script, you might lose access to the input devices unless you hard reset the computer. Don't worry, "pyautogui" provides pause and failsafe features. "Failsafe" is triggered when the mouse hits the top right corner of the screen and device control is returned to the user. The "pause" creates a delay so you can stop the program execution if need be. Note that once you lose control of your keyboard, you won't be able to use the CTRL+C to break the program execution.

```
import pyautogui

pyautogui.FAILSAFE = True

pyautogui.PAUSE = 1
```

Before we automate the keyboard or mouse, we need to know what is the size of the screen so we would know the limits.

```
pyautogui.size()
```

Mouse automation

```
for xy in range(8):

    pyautogui.moveTo(50, 50, duration=0.5)

    pyautogui.moveTo(100, 50, duration=0.5)

    pyautogui.moveTo(100, 100, duration=0.5)

    pyautogui.moveTo(50, 100, duration=0.5)
```

The above code moves the mouse cursor in a square shape pattern in the clockwise direction. Each movement will occur in 0.25 seconds so it will be visible for you to see the movement. In the above example, we have used fixed coordinates. We can use relative coordinates also, just like we have used below.

pyautogui.moveRel(50, 50, duration=0.5)

All this wouldn't make sense if we don't know what the current position of the cursor is.

pyautogui.position()

We can also automate mouse click like this.

pyautogui.click(7, 3)

We have to provide fixed coordinates to the click() method, not relative. The click() method mimics the left mouse button being pressed and released. We can use "pyautogui.mouseDown()" and "pyautogui,mouseUp()" to automate either pressing or releasing of the mouse button. The "pyautogui.doubleClick()" simulates a double click. You can use "pyautogui.rightClick()" to simulate a right click and a middle button click with "pyautogui.middleClick()".

There are two methods "pyautogui,dragTo()" and "pyautogui.dragRel()" to automate dragging, both of which work in a similar manner as moveTo() and moveRel() methods we have seen before. The difference is that with drag modules, the mouse button is also left clicked to force a drag instead of just moving the cursor.

Newer mice come with the scrolling wheel and it can be automated too with the scroll() method. You have to pass an integer value that pyatuogui uses to determine how much the screen has to move up or down. The integer values will result in different scroll movement on different screen sizes and computer systems. One important thing to remember: the scroll() method is relative, which means the scrolling will start from the current position of the mouse.

We can also take a screenshot with "pyautogui" library using the screenshot() method.

viewfreeze = pyautogui.screenshot()

Keyboard automation

Keyboard actions can be simulated using the rhe "pyautogui.typewrite()" method. Depending upon the application currently active, the same key presses might result in different actions. Here is an example of typing a string with each keystroke happening after a delay.

pyautogui.typewrite("Dora The Explorer!", 0.71)

We can also automate keyboard actions such as adding a new line by passing a special code in the typewrite(). Here's a table of codes assigned to different keyboard actions.

Key string	Meaning
'a', 'b', 'c', 'A', 'B', 'C', '1', '2', '3', '!', '@', '#', and so on	keys for single characters
'enter' (or 'return'or '\n')	ENTER key
'esc'	ESC key
'shiftleft', 'shiftright'	Left and Right SHIFT keys
'altleft','altright'	Left and Right ALT keys
'ctrlleft','ctrlright'	Left and Right CTRL keys
'tab' or '\t'	TAB key
'backspace','delete'	BACKSPACE and DELETE keys
'pageup','pagedown'	PAGE UP and PAGE DOWN keys

'home','end'	HOME and END keys
'up','down','left','right'	ARROW keys
'f1','f2','f3' and so on...	F1 to F12 keys
'volumeup','volumedown','mute'	VOLUME control keys. Your keyboard might have these keys but you r system might still be able to recognize these commands
'pause'	PAUSE key
'capslock','numlock','scrolllock'	LOCK keys
'insert'	INSERT or INS key
'printscreen'	PRINT SCREEN or PRTSC key
'winleft','winright'	Left and Right WIN keys (Windows only)

We can combine different keypresses to type a special character. The following lines of code result in '%' getting typed.

```
pyautogui.keyDown('shift')
```

```
pyautogui.press('5')
```

```
pyautogui.keyUp('shift')
```

The hotkey() method is very useful because we can perform system operations like copy and paste by mimicking the simultaneous press of CTRL and another key. For example, here is how we can automate a copy command.

```
pyautogui.hotkey('ctrl','c')
```

Chapter 8: Gaming with Python

Gaming is not new, it's as old as the computers. It's one of the biggest industries related to computers and programming in terms of revenue and salaries. With the advent of smartphones, more and more independent developers are launching games in the hope of hitting the jackpot. The codes in the chapter are inspired by the work of Youtube channel "techwithtim".

Python provides a way to create 2D games and we are going to take a look at it now.

PyGame Introduction

The "pygame" is an excellent external library for building games. Let's install "pygame".

pip install pygame

The following code shows the basics of setting up a game environment. Comments are added to explain important points.

import pygame

pygame.init() # start the gaming engine

win = pygame.display.set_mode((500, 500)) # This line creates a window of 500 width, 500 height

pygame.display.set_caption("First Game") # change window name

Initializing the character attributes.

x = 50

y = 50

width = 40

height = 60

vel = 5

setting an infinite loop

run = True

```python
while run:

    pygame.time.delay(100)


    for event in pygame.event.get():

        if event.type == pygame.QUIT:

            run = False # end game loop only in this condition


    keys = pygame.key.get_pressed() # check if a keyboard key is pressed and which
key it is

    # move the character wrt to the keyboard key pressed

    if keys[pygame.K_LEFT]:

        x -= vel


    if keys[pygame.K_RIGHT]:

        x += vel


    if keys[pygame.K_UP]:

        y -= vel


    if keys[pygame.K_DOWN]:

        y += vel


    win.fill((0,0,0))  # Fills the screen with black so there's no tail of the character
```

```
pygame.draw.rect(win, (255,0,0), (x, y, width, height)) # draw the character

pygame.display.update() # update the display on every loop execution
```

```
pygame.quit() # stop the game when loop is broken
```

Creating a 2D Game

We are going to create the popular Tetris game that will become more difficult over time.

Part #1: Initialization

We have to create the game environment before we can start coding the mechanics and other details. Here's the complete code that initializes the Tetris game environment. Comments are added where necessary to describe certain aspects.

```
import pygame

import random



# creating the data structure for pieces

# setting up global vars

# functions

# - create_grid

# - draw_grid

# - draw_window

# - rotating shape in main

# - setting up the main
```

```
"""

10 x 20 square grid

shapes: S, Z, I, O, J, L, T

represented in order by 0 - 6

"""


pygame.font.init()


# GLOBALS VARS

s_width = 800

s_height = 700

play_width = 300  # meaning 300 // 10 = 30 width per block

play_height = 600  # meaning 600 // 20 = 20 height per block

block_size = 30


top_left_x = (s_width - play_width) // 2

top_left_y = s_height - play_height



# SHAPE FORMATS


S = [['.....',
     '......',
```

```
    '..00.',

    '.00..',

    '.....'],

   ['.....',

    '..0..',

    '..00.',

    '...0.',

    '.....']]


Z = [['.....',

    '.....',

    '.00..',

    '..00.',

    '.....'],

   ['.....',

    '..0..',

    '.00..',

    '.0...',

    '.....']]


I = [['..0..',

    '..0..',

    '..0..',
```

```
   '..0..',
   '.....'],
  ['.....',
   '0000.',
   '.....',
   '.....',
   '.....']]


O = [['.....',
   '.....',
   '.00..',
   '.00..',
   '.....']]


J = [['.....',
   '.0...',
   '.000.',
   '.....',
   '.....'],
  ['.....',
   '..00.',
   '..0..',
   '..0..',
```

```
     '.....'],

    ['.....',

     '.....',

     '.000.',

     '...0.',

     '.....'],

    ['.....',

     '..0..',

     '..0..',

     '.00..',

     '.....']]


L = [['.....',

     '...0.',

     '.000.',

     '.....',

     '.....'],

    ['.....',

     '..0..',

     '..0..',

     '..00.',

     '.....'],

    ['.....',
```

```
        '.....',

        '.000.',

        '.0...',

        '.....'],

      ['.....',

        '.00..',

        '..0..',

        '..0..',

        '.....']]


T = [['.....',

        '..0..',

        '.000.',

        '.....',

        '.....'],

      ['.....',

        '..0..',

        '..00.',

        '..0..',

        '.....'],

      ['.....',

        '.....',

        '.000.',
```

```
    '..0..',

    '.....'],

   ['.....',

    '..0..',

    '.00..',

    '..0..',

    '.....']]


shapes = [S, Z, I, O, J, L, T]

shape_colors = [(0, 255, 0), (255, 0, 0), (0, 255, 255), (255, 255, 0), (255, 165, 0), (0, 0,
255), (128, 0, 128)]

# index 0 - 6 represent shape




class Piece(object):

    pass




def create_grid(locked_positions={}):

    pass




def convert_shape_format(shape):

    pass




def valid_space(shape, grid):
```

```python
        pass


def check_lost(positions):

    pass


def get_shape():

    pass


def draw_text_middle(text, size, color, surface):

    pass


def draw_grid(surface, row, col):

    pass


def clear_rows(grid, locked):

    pass


def draw_next_shape(shape, surface):

    pass


def draw_window(surface):

    pass
```

```python
def main():

    pass


def main_menu():

    pass



main_menu()  # start game
```

Part #2: Game Design

I have divided the code into various sections for easier understanding. You need to keep all this code in one script file.

Class for Piece Shapes

We are going to create different shapes and it's better to create a class for all shapes that defines all the common properties and functions.

```python
class Piece(object):

    rows = 20  # y

    columns = 10  # x


    def __init__(self, column, row, shape):

        self.x = column

        self.y = row

        self.shape = shape

        self.color = shape_colors[shapes.index(shape)]

        self.rotation = 0  # number from 0-3
```

Create a Game Grid

This piece of code creates the visible gaming area. The randomly generated shapes will occupy this grid according to the user input.

```python
def create_grid(locked_positions={}):

    grid = [[(0,0,0) for x in range(10)] for x in range(20)]


    for i in range(len(grid)):

        for j in range(len(grid[i])):

            if (j,i) in locked_positions:

                c = locked_positions[(j,i)]

                grid[i][j] = c

    return grid
```

Randomizing Shape Generation

This code generates different shapes randomly. Note that we already set all the shapes that will be generated during initialization.

```python
def get_shape():

    global shapes, shape_colors


    return Piece(5, 0, random.choice(shapes))
```

Game Grid Build

This part of script builds the grid where the game will be played.

```python
surface.fill((0,0,0))

    # Tetris Title

    font = pygame.font.SysFont('comicsans', 60)

    label = font.render('TETRIS', 1, (255,255,255))
```

```
surface.blit(label, (top_left_x + play_width / 2 - (label.get_width() / 2), 30))


    for i in range(len(grid)):

        for j in range(len(grid[i])):

            pygame.draw.rect(surface, grid[i][j], (top_left_x + j* 30, top_left_y + i * 30, 30,
30), 0)



    # draw grid and border

    draw_grid(surface, 20, 10)

    pygame.draw.rect(surface, (255, 0, 0), (top_left_x, top_left_y, play_width,
play_height), 5)

    pygame.display.update()
```

Create Game Loop

This is the main loop that will be constantly running looking for events and invoking necessary actions. The "while" loop helps create an infinite iteration that will only break if we lose or win the game.

```
def main():

    global grid


    locked_positions = {}  # (x,y):(255,0,0)

    grid = create_grid(locked_positions)


    change_piece = False

    run = True

    current_piece = get_shape()

    next_piece = get_shape()
```

```python
    clock = pygame.time.Clock()

    fall_time = 0


    while run:

        for event in pygame.event.get():

            if event.type == pygame.QUIT:

                run = False

                pygame.display.quit()

                quit()


            if event.type == pygame.KEYDOWN:

                if event.key == pygame.K_LEFT:

                    current_piece.x -= 1

                    if not valid_space(current_piece, grid):

                        current_piece.x += 1


                elif event.key == pygame.K_RIGHT:

                    current_piece.x += 1

                    if not valid_space(current_piece, grid):

                        current_piece.x -= 1

                elif event.key == pygame.K_UP:

                    # rotate shape

                    current_piece.rotation = current_piece.rotation + 1 %
len(current_piece.shape)
```

```
        if not valid_space(current_piece, grid):

            current_piece.rotation = current_piece.rotation - 1 %
len(current_piece.shape)


    if event.key == pygame.K_DOWN:

        # move shape down

        current_piece.y += 1

        if not valid_space(current_piece, grid):

            current_piece.y -= 1



    draw_window(win)
```

Part #3: Building the Game

Add Visuals to the Game Grid

We are going to add grid lines so players will know how much space a shape takes and how much the shape can be moved.

```
def draw_grid(surface, row, col):

# This function draws the grey grid lines that we see

  sx = top_left_x

  sy = top_left_y

  for i in range(row):

      pygame.draw.line(surface, (128,128,128), (sx, sy+ i*30), (sx + play_width, sy + i *
30))  # horizontal lines

      for j in range(col):

          pygame.draw.line(surface, (128,128,128), (sx + j * 30, sy), (sx + j * 30, sy +
play_height))  # vertical lines
```

Track Position of Shape in the Grid

During the game, we must be able to track the position of the shapes. Here's the code to do that.

```
def convert_shape_format(shape):

    positions = []

    format = shape.shape[shape.rotation % len(shape.shape)]


    for i, line in enumerate(format):

        row = list(line)

        for j, column in enumerate(row):

            if column == \'0\':

                positions.append((shape.x + j, shape.y + i))


    for i, pos in enumerate(positions):

        positions[i] = (pos[0] - 2, pos[1] - 4)


    return positions
```

Check if Certain Grid Space is Valid

To make sure the shape doesn't move into a space that's already taken or is out of the available grid, we have to write a function. Here's the code to check grid space validity.

```
def valid_space(shape, grid):

    accepted_positions = [[(j, i) for j in range(10) if grid[i][j] == (0,0,0)] for i in range(20)]

    accepted_positions = [j for sub in accepted_positions for j in sub]

    formatted = convert_shape_format(shape)
```

```
    for pos in formatted:

      if pos not in accepted_positions:

        if pos[1] > -1:

          return False


  return True
```

Check if Game is Lost

We have to constantly check if user has lost the game. Here's the function code to check that.

```
def check_lost(positions):

  for pos in positions:

    x, y = pos

    if y < 1:

      return True

  return False
```

Modify Game Loop

Remember we created the main game loop in Part #2? We need to add more codes to it. Add the following code block right after the "while run:" line.

```
fall_speed = 0.27


    grid = create_grid(locked_positions)

    fall_time += clock.get_rawtime()

    clock.tick()
```

147

```
# PIECE FALLING CODE

if fall_time/1000 >= fall_speed:

    fall_time = 0

    current_piece.y += 1

    if not (valid_space(current_piece, grid)) and current_piece.y > 0:

        current_piece.y -= 1

        change_piece = True
```

Before the "draw_window(win, grid)" line, add the following lines of code.

```
shape_pos = convert_shape_format(current_piece)


    # add color of piece to the grid for drawing

    for i in range(len(shape_pos)):

        x, y = shape_pos[i]

        if y > -1: # If we are not above the screen

            grid[y][x] = current_piece.color

    # IF PIECE HIT GROUND

    if change_piece:

        for pos in shape_pos:

            p = (pos[0], pos[1])

            locked_positions[p] = current_piece.color

        current_piece = next_piece

        next_piece = get_shape()

        change_piece = False
```

After the "draw_window(win, grid)" line, add the following lines of code.

```
# Check if user lost

    if check_lost(locked_positions):

        run = False
```

Part #4: Adding Features to The Game

Show Next Shape on the Side

We want to show the next shape that will enter the grid from the top on the right side of the grid. Here's a function to do that.

```
def draw_next_shape(shape, surface):

    font = pygame.font.SysFont('comicsans', 30)

    label = font.render('Next Shape', 1, (255,255,255))



    sx = top_left_x + play_width + 50

    sy = top_left_y + play_height/2 - 100

    format = shape.shape[shape.rotation % len(shape.shape)]



    for i, line in enumerate(format):

        row = list(line)

        for j, column in enumerate(row):

            if column == '0':

                pygame.draw.rect(surface, shape.color, (sx + j*30, sy + i*30, 30, 30), 0)



    surface.blit(label, (sx + 10, sy- 30))
```

We need to call this function in the main() so it will constantly run.

This should go inside the while loop right BELOW draw_window()

Near the end of the loop

draw_next_shape(next_piece, win)

pygame.display.update()

Clear Filled Row

When a grid row is completely filled, it must be removed from the grid and all other rows shifted down. Here's the function code to do that.

```
def clear_rows(grid, locked):

    # need to see if row is clear then shift every other row above down one


    inc = 0

    for i in range(len(grid)-1,-1,-1):

        row = grid[i]

        if (0, 0, 0) not in row:

            inc += 1

            # add positions to remove from locked

            ind = i

            for j in range(len(row)):

                try:

                    del locked[(j, i)]

                except:

                    continue

    if inc > 0:
```

```
    for key in sorted(list(locked), key=lambda x: x[1])[::-1]:

        x, y = key

        if y < ind:

            newKey = (x, y + inc)

            locked[newKey] = locked.pop(key)
```

We also need to call this function from the main() function. Add the following lines of code at the end of "if change_piece:" block.

```
# call four times to check for multiple clear rows

    clear_rows(grid, locked_positions) # < ---------- GOES HERE
```

Part #5: Raise Difficulty

In a Tetris game, we can increase the game difficulty by increasing the speed with which the shapes fall down the grid.

In the main() function, just before the "while run:" line, add the following line of code.

```
level_time = 0
```

Now, add the following line of code at the start of "while run:" loop.

```
level_time += clock.get_rawtime()
```

```
  if level_time/1000 > 5:

    level_time = 0

    if level_time > 0.12:

      level_time -= 0.005
```

Part #6: Game Build

The following lines of code will go at the end of the script.

```
win = pygame.display.set_mode((s_width, s_height))
pygame.display.set_caption(\'Tetris\')

main()
```

We can add many more features to the game to offer a better gaming experience. Here are some ideas:

1. Add a scoring system. For example, award 10 points for each filled row cleared from the grid
2. Add a main menu to the game
3. Add an exit screen with score etc. summary after the game stops running

The above example is just the beginning when it comes to creating games with Python. Well-known games including Battlefield 2 and The Sims 4 utilize the power of Python to create a highly immersive gaming experience. If you want to become a game developer and don't have the capital to invest in proprietary platforms, Python can help you become famous!

Creating an Executable Distribution of Software

We have to install an external library to create distributable ".exe" package for any Python script.

```
pip install pyinstaller
```

Using the command prompt, navigate to the directory where the Python script is present. Let's say our script file name is "appComp.py". We have to run the following command.

```
pyinstaller --onefile appComp.py
```

The process can take a few minutes to complete depending upon your script. It automatically takes care of any libraries you added in the script. Once it's finished, a few new folders and files will be present in the folder where your Python script was present. Open the "dist" folder and you will see the "appComp.exe" file. Easy!

Conclusion

Python has created a revolution in the programming world due to its open source nature. The rise of data analysis and machine learning have also made Python very relevant. It offers easier syntax but doesn't compromise in power or speed. All these qualities have made the language ideal for people who are not programmers but want to create scripts to achieve specific objectives.

Python 2.7 is the most popular version even though the support is going to end very soon. Code written in Python 2.7 is not forward compatible with Python 3.0. It definitely created a dilemma for companies who have relied on Python for years. It's not easy to port millions of lines of code. Due to this reason, Python 2.7 End of Life (EOL) has been extended several times. But, it's certain it will not be extended this time.

There are various books and YouTube channels that you can refer to if you want to build upon the skills learned in this book. Python is a great programming language if you want to freelance or start your own programming firm. I hope your Python journey is fun and full of rewards!

References

Eric Matthes, Python Crash Course, 2nd edition. San Francisco, CA: No Starch Press Inc., 2019.

James R. Parker, Python: An Introduction to Programming. Dulles, VA: Mercury Learning and Information, 2017.

Ryan Turner, Python Programming: 3 Books in 1: Ultimate Beginner's, Intermediate & Advanced Guide to Learn Python Step-by-Step. James C Anderson, 2018.

Steven Samelson, Python Programming: A Step-by-Step Guide From Absolute Beginners to Complete Guide for Intermediates and Advanced. Steven Samelson, 2019.

Python for data science

Introduction

You have taken the first step on your path to learning data science by purchasing *Python for Data Science: The ultimate python guide for beginners. Python machine learning tools, concepts and introduction. Python programming crash course.* Allow yourself to be guided in the field of data science step by step from the very beginning with the help of this book. The purpose of *Python for Data Science* is to educate the complete beginner on the fundamental topics of data science.

Studying this field can be exhausting, difficult and even intimidating to some, especially those with limited programming knowledge. Fortunately, the step by step approach of this book will teach you the theory as well as the practical skills you need to implement learning algorithms and techniques on your own in no time. All you need is a desire to learn and a good instruction manual with a practical approach towards study.

This book includes the following topics:

- In the first chapter you learn how to setup your Python work environment by creating a virtual environment where you will install a scientific distribution that includes all of the tools you need. Keep in mind that you will be working only with free tools and open source datasets, so you won't have to pay a dime.
- Once your toolkit is ready, the next two chapters will teach you about the importance of data pre-processing and exploration. Do not rush through these sections because the more time and effort you invest in preparing your data, the better results you will obtain.
- Once your data is prepared, you will begin exploring a variety of supervised and unsupervised learning algorithms and techniques. You will learn about linear regression, the Naïve Bayes classifier, the K-nearest neighbor algorithm, support vector machines, decision trees, K-means clustering and more.
- After learning the fundamental learning techniques you will start exploring the power of neural networks. These structures are some of the most powerful data analysis techniques in data science, and this chapter will introduce you to the most popular ones. You will learn about a variety of neural networks such as the single layer and multilayer perceptron, as well as the Restricted Boltzmann Machine.
- Finally, you will also be introduced to the field of Big Data, which is a subfield of data science that processes vast volumes of data. You will learn why this subfield is the future and what real world applications exist for it. Furthermore, you will gain an idea about which supervised and unsupervised learning algorithms can be used when handling Big Data.

Take note that in order to learn fast and benefit from this guide, you need to practice along with it. It is very tempting to start reading and not let go of the book, however, doing things that way means you won't learn much. The book is divided in such a way that it allows you to go section by section, bit by bit, and make your way up the ladder until you understand the fundamentals of data science. And make sure to practice every concept and technique!

Chapter 1: Getting Started

Data science is a relatively new discipline that has entered the market only recently. Even though this field has existed for decades, it was only studied and researched mostly on a theoretical level by mathematicians and specialists from various technical fields. Data science includes a number of components that can be studied individually as well, such as machine learning, computational linguistics, data analysis, linear algebra and many more. From these elements alone we can conclude that data science is in fact a seemingly chaotic mixture of mathematics, programming, and data communication. However, this combination is one of the main reasons why data science is so widely used for a variety of purposes. It is a versatile field. This versatility, however, leads to a number of different specialties destined for certain areas of expertise within data science.

But before we discuss what data science is in detail, you should understand what it isn't. Many beginners get the wrong idea about this field and they end up making mistakes that can set them back on their journey.

First of all, know that data science is not equal to software development or engineering. Your job as a future data scientist will not be developing products, systems, or features. Secondly, data science is not about graphical work, or visualization. You will not develop tools focusing on cool visuals or graphical elements. Thirdly, data science does not involve scientific work in the sense of academia. The field is determined by what the industry or market requires from the data scientist. Finally, there is a false image of data science involving mostly statistics. The field of statistical analysis and anything related to that subject can be part of data science and having that kind of knowledge can prove to be useful, however, there is far more to it than that. Statistical knowledge alone will not qualify you to become a data scientist.

With that in mind, let's now discuss what data science actually is. This field involves programming skills, statistical understanding, visualization concepts, and finally a business sense. This last component may often be harder to acquire, however, it is just as important as the others, if not more so. When we refer to a business sense we are discussing the ability to answer any possible business questions with all the available data you are provided with. You need to be capable of connecting the dots by using only the carefully selected data from a world full of data. Essentially, the data scientist is the one who connects the world of business with the technical world of data.

To keep it simple for now, data science can be compared to cooking. You start preparing your ingredients first by cleaning the vegetables, the meat, and chop everything to the desired size. In the same way you start the data science process through data munging, which involves data cleansing, debugging, extraction, loading and so on. Once this step is completed, you start cooking your ingredients, step by step, timing every process until the raw food can be eaten. This step corresponds to data exploration and various processes such as feature reduction or construction. Now the meal is ready to be served and you arrange it nicely on your plate in order for it to be nice and presentable, and you serve everything in a specific sequence. In data science this final step is the part where you display your data mining results, perhaps with the aid of graphical visualization in order to make it easy for your business users to understand the data reports.

Now that you have an idea about the ingredients behind the cooking process, you need to obtain the right set of tools. Developing a professional toolkit from the beginning is a crucial step. In the field of data science you will always be learning new techniques and add to your toolkit. However, there is one tool that serves as the foundation for everything else, and that is Python.

Python is one of the best multi-purpose tools in data science, as well as other technical specializations. In this case, it is particularly powerful when it comes to data munging, as well as data mining, especially with the help of packages and libraries such as Scikit-learn. However, it's worth mentioning that sometimes R is used as the alternative, however, it is somewhat lacking when it comes to data munging. It is often used as a way to prototype your data science problem because of its usefulness when undergoing data exploration or testing algorithms under different conditions.

In this book, we are going to focus on Python due to its simplicity, power, versatility and ability to be extended with a variety of open source libraries and packages. This programming language is used in many fields, as it's becoming increasingly impossible to work with computers without hearing about Python. Some people consider it nothing but a trend for beginners, however, that's not the case as it is used in everything from software development to machine learning and data science by everyone whether a complete novice or professional.

Python's humble beginnings are found in 1991 when Guido van Rossum, a big fan of the famous Monty Python comedy group, designed it. Speaking of comedy, if you are a fan yourself, keep your eyes open as you go through the documentation for this language and you'll find several fun Easter eggs. With that bit of trivia out of the way, here are some of the main characteristics that make Python the optimal choice for studying data science:

1. Python is powerful: This programming language can equip you with every tool you need for every step you need to perform and it won't cost you a thing. Being an open source product has its advantages. Developers from around the world continue to improve and refine the language, especially with the addition of various packages, libraries, and modules. Python is more powerful than ever before because of how much its usability can be extended.
2. Python is versatile and user friendly: This feature is tied to the first one in many ways. First of all, Python is one of the most beginner-friendly programming languages you can learn and that is why it is often recommended for aspiring data scientists and machine learners. All you need is a basic grasp on the language and then you can focus on the data science concepts and techniques. Secondly, the ability to extend the language makes it easier for you to work with algorithms, especially if you are a complete beginner.
3. Python is easy to integrate: Many other tools and even programming languages can be used in combination with Python. For instance, if you

know how to code in C or C++, you can use that language for the bulk of your programming tasks and then use Python as the central hub which connects all your tools to your code.

4. Python is compatible with many platforms: Portability is sometimes a problem, especially when you work on one system to achieve your goals and then you have to move your entire work to a different system. This is where Python excels. The code and the tools you work with using Python will automatically run on any operating system, whether it's Windows, Linux or Mac.

To summarize, Python is powerful, easy to learn and even master, and can be integrated with a variety of tools, programming languages as well as operating systems. With that being said, let's dive in and start installing Python, as well as all the other tools we will need.

Python Setup

In this section we are going to discuss the installation process for Python, as well as a number of its extensions. If you are already familiar with the programming language, you can skip the setup and continue reading about libraries and scientific distributions. If this is the first time you are installing it, however, you should know that Python comes in two different versions. You have the option to install Python 2 or Python 3. As you can probably tell, version 2 is the older one, however, it is still in use and many data scientists choose to stick with it for the time being. Read up on the documentation and perhaps check what the online Python community has to say as well and then decide which version to use. Some tools and extensions work only with Python 2, so keep that in mind as well.

In this book we are going to focus on the up to date Python 3 because this version is the future and it will continue receiving support for quite some time. Whatever your decision is, please stick to one of them all the way in order to avoid any compatibility issues. If you write your code in Python 2 and then you execute it in a system that runs with Python 3, you might encounter serious errors.

With that in mind, head to Python's official webpage at www.python.org and download your chosen version of Python for the operating system your computer is using. Keep in mind that for the purpose of data science, installing Python alone is not enough. Therefore, you have two options. You can either install everything manually and select each element and tool as needed, or install a Python scientific distribution, which essentially is a package that contains everything you need. Nonetheless, we are going to discuss both methods because having full control over what is needed for your project is important.

Once you downloaded Python, simply follow the instructions to perform the basic setup. Now, you need to also install a variety of packages, otherwise the language alone with its base components isn't that useful for data science. To perform this step manually, you need to use a package manager. Fortunately, Python comes with one already installed and it's called "pip". Open you command terminal and type pip in order to launch the manager. This package manager will allow you to install and uninstall any component whenever you wish. You can even perform updates to every single package, or only to certain ones. You even have the option of rolling back to a different version if the update causes some kind of conflicts within your project. With that being said, let's install a package by typing this command:

pip install < myPackage >

That's it! You only need to know the name of the package you want to install and use its name as a keyword. Updating and removing the packages is done the same way. Simply replace the "install" keyword with the appropriate one for each command.

Now that you have an idea about the basic installation process, let's discuss scientific distributions. Installing and maintaining dozens of packages and modules by hand can be quite tedious, so let's automate it.

Python Scientific Distributions

Creating your Python working environment can be time consuming and can lead to compatibility errors if you go through the process manually. Some tools don't work well together, or they require the installation of certain dependencies you aren't aware of. It is good to be able to customize your Python installation, however, as a beginner you might want to stick to a Python distribution instead.

Save your time and effort to practice data science and machine learning concepts and techniques instead of fiddling with various packages. A scientific distribution will allow you to automate the entire installation process, finish it within minutes and then jump straight into practical data science. There are different scientific distributions out there and they each contain a certain set of tools designed for various types of projects. However, they all have in common the fact that they contain a number of powerful Python libraries, specifically designed with data science in mind, as well as an Integrated Development Environment and other tools to get you started as soon as possible. With that being said, let's discuss the most important distributions that you should download and explore.

Anaconda

One of the most popular scientific distributions you can find is Anaconda. In a way it completes Python by extending it with around 200 pre-installed packages that include the ones data scientists use the most, such as NumPy, Pandas, Matplotlib and Scikit-learn. Furthermore, Anaconda can run on any computer no matter which operating system and version you're running and can even be installed next to other distributions without causing any conflicts.

This scientific distribution contains everything you need, especially in the beginning of your journey. It offers you all the tools needed to perform data analyses and explorations, as well as mass data processing and computing. In addition, it comes with its own package manager, which allows you to tweak the packages yourself or maintain them manually if you prefer. However, the most attractive part about using Anaconda is the fact that it offers you all of that for free, while other distributions might involve certain fees.

If you decided to go with Anaconda, you will need to get accustomed to its internal package manager which is accessed with the keyword "conda". The manager works just like pip and is used to install, delete, or update any or all of your packages. Furthermore, it can also be used to setup a virtual environment (we'll discuss it soon). Now, let's check to see if we are running the most recent version of conda before we do anything else. Perform the verification and update by simply using the update keyword like so:

conda update conda

Now, in order to manually install certain packages, because the distribution might not contain quite everything you need, you need to use the install keyword just like you did when testing out the pip package manager. You can even install several packages at the same time by simply listing them all in a sequence. Here's how that looks like in the command console:

conda install < package1> < package2 > < package3 > < package100 >

Next, you can update the packages with the update function. The easiest way to do this is to simply update everything at once by adding the "—all" keyword. Here's how:

conda update –all

Lastly, you might want to remove some of the packages you don't need, or if you installed one that causes some kind of conflicts with another package. Simply use the "remove" keyword to instruct the manager to remove the desired package. It's that simple.

Conda is a very intuitive package manager and it is easy to use. If you discover that you prefer it over other managers like pip, then you can even install it separately to use it with any other scientific distributions.

Now, let's explore another scientific distribution called Canopy.

Canopy

This distribution is a popular alternative to Anaconda because its aim is to provide data scientists and analysts with all the tools they need to do their job. It also contains approximately 200 packages, including Pandas and Matplotlib. Make sure to check the distribution's documentation to see all the other packages it contains because they are too numerous to list here.

In many ways Canopy is similar to Anaconda. They both have many packages in common, however, without paying a fee you will only have basic access to Canopy. For starters that's enough, however, if you ever need its advanced features you need to install the main version of the distribution.

WinPython

This distribution is aimed at Windows users, as the name suggests. Essentially, it offers you the same features as Anaconda and Canopy, however, while the others have paid versions with more advanced features, this distribution is entirely community driven and therefore free. WinPython is an open source tool that you are free to use however you want and you can even modify it yourself if you have the required skills to do so.

The main drawback of course is the fact that it can be installed only on a Windows machine, but if you do use one, you should consider it because it even allows you to install several versions of it on the same computer. In addition it also offers you a free IDE.

Virtual Environments

Now that you have an idea about scientific distributions, let's take a sidestep and discuss the power of virtual environments before exploring various Python libraries and other tools you need.

Virtual environments are one of the most useful tools when practicing something new, or when you want to be able to perform multiple tasks in different environments. Keep in mind that you are normally restricted by your operating system or by the version of Python which you currently installed on your system. No matter the chosen installation method, it is difficult to install different versions of the same tools without risking potential software conflicts and errors. However, if you take the virtual environment route, you will have a number of advantages and no significant disadvantages.

One of the biggest benefits of working through a virtual environment is the fact that it can be your testing ground. This means that you can dedicate an area of your system to experimentation and learning without any consequences. You can try any variety of libraries, modules, different versions of your tools and so on. Furthermore, you can learn and practice data science concepts and techniques without being worried that you will damage your system in some way. Eliminate the stress of having to reinstall your operating system or fix complicated errors by learning to work through a virtual environment. The worst case involves resetting the environment, which means you don't need to Google obscure error codes or try to fix your operating system because you messed something up.

Studying aside, another reason why so many choose to work through a virtual environment is because it allows them to have multiple Python and data science distributions installed at the same time. In addition, you can also install multiple versions of your operating system to see how your project behaves. You can even install different operating systems altogether on the same machine without affecting your main system. Some of the packages and modules work only with certain versions of Python for instance. Therefore you can use a virtual environment for Python version 2 and another one for Python version 3. Create unique virtual environments that suit your needs precisely.

Finally, a virtual environment will help you verify the replicability of your project. Sometimes you need to make sure that whatever task you performed or project you worked on can be replicated on a different operating system or with a different Python version. By installing different versions of your tools or the operating system in separate virtual environments you can test your prototype and see how it performs.

Now that you understand what virtual environments are for, let's install one with pip:

pip install virtualenv

Installation is quite straightforward, however, you will need to make some considerations at the end of the setup. For instance, you will need to decide which version of Python your virtual environment should use. The default version is the one from which virtualenv is installed. Next, you need to consider your packages. With each virtual environment installation, all of the packages will also be installed. This is a good thing because it's one less task you need to perform, however, when you setup multiple virtual environments each one of them will install the same packages once again. This is a waste of system resources, as well as time. There is no need to install the same thing more than once, therefore you need to issue a command for the virtual environment to use the files it already has access to instead of installing a new set. Finally, you need to consider whether you need the option to relocate your virtual environment to a different system that perhaps even uses a different version of Python. To make your virtual environment relocation-friendly, you need to specify that you want the scripts to work no matter the path.

Once you choose the correct options for your situation, you can finally create and launch the environment. Type this line to generate the new environment:

virtualenv myEnv

A new virtual environment will be created together with a directory named "myEnv" where it will reside. Now let's launch the environment with these commands:

cd myEnv

activate

The environment is now ready and we can install all of the tools we need as before. The environment acts exactly the same as your system so everything you did so far you can do in any virtual environment you create.

Data Science Packages

So far we kept mentioning how powerful Python is because of the wide variety of packages, libraries, and extensions that we have access to specifically for data science and analytics. As a beginner data scientist you will need to understand these packages because they represent your toolkit without which your knowledge can't be easily applied.

In this section we are going to briefly explore the most important Python packages and tools you will be working with throughout this book. Keep in mind that these tools have been selected because they are industry standard, polished, and frequently updated, and most importantly well-documented.

1. Scikit-learn: This is one of the most important tools used by data scientists, analysts, machine learners, and software engineers. This is a free Python library that contains some of the algorithms that you will frequently use, such as classification, clustering, and regression algorithms. They include k-means clustering, support vector machines, random forests, gradient boosting and many more. Furthermore, this library is designed to be used with other libraries, such as the Python numerical library known as NumPy and the scientific library known as SciPy. In order to install the library, simply type *pip install scikit-learn*. Remember to replace pip with the keyword for your chosen package manager, if you prefer a different one.

2. NumPy: This library goes hand in hand with Scikit-learn due to the support it offers for multi-dimensional arrays. This includes various algorithms that operate purely on these arrays which are used for data storage and certain matrix operations. The reason why we need this Python extension is because the programming language wasn't initially designed for numerical computing operations. Since complex mathematical operations are part of any data scientist's daily work, NumPy is a must-have.

3. SciPy: NumPy and SciPy are frequently used together because they fill each other's weak points. This open source library is used for technical and scientific computing processes. It adds modules to Python that are used for optimization, interpolation, linear algebra, image processing and much more. The reason why SciPy compliments NumPy is because it builds on the array object that is part of the NumPy library. Furthermore, it also expands on other libraries and tools such as Matplotlit and Pandas.

4. Pandas: This Python library was created mainly for manipulating data as well as analyzing it. Its most important features include data structures and operations that are needed to manipulate tables, as well as time series.

Take note that Pandas is also free software and that it has nothing to do with pandas. The name of the library refers to "panel data", which describes data sets that involve a set of observations over a number of recorded time periods.

5. Matplotlib: Sometimes you might want to sit back and visualize your data without looking at confusing numbers to form a conclusion. Sometimes you have to present your findings to those who are not technically inclined and do not understand raw numbers. In either case you would benefit from using plots to build a graphical representation of your findings. This is what Matplotlib is for. It allows you to build plots by using an array and then visualize the data, including interactively. In case you don't know what a plot is, it is a graph that is often used in statistical analysis in order to demonstrate a connection between certain variables.

6. Jupyter: Finally, we have Jupyter which will act as your data science IDE. It is often used by machine learners and data scientists because of how user-friendly it is and because it works with any programming language. However, the most important aspect is the fact that it allows you to visualize your data straight in the environment instead of opening new windows or panels and being forced to switch them. You write your code, your algorithms, and look at your data. In addition, Jupyter also provides you with the ability to directly communicate with other users and collaborate with them by sharing project files. We will discuss Jupyter in a bit more detail soon.

These Python tools should be more than enough for a beginner data scientist. You may feel overwhelmed, especially when you consider there are hundreds of packages and libraries that you will eventually use. However, for now, you should stick to the tools that form the foundation of nearly every project.

Before moving on, let's discuss one more component which we mentioned only briefly, namely Jupyter. This tool forms your development environment and you will use it for every project. If you are used to the usual IDE's that are designed with programming and software development in mind, like Atom and Visual Studio, you will notice that Jupyter is quite different and you might even feel a bit lost. Therefore, let's take a moment to discuss using this environment.

Jupyter

All the concepts and techniques you will practice with the help of this book will be done using Jupyter. In order to install it, all you need to do is download it and use the install command with your chosen package manager. The setup itself is very easy to follow, so just perform every step as requested by the installer. If you encounter any errors, then you probably downloaded the wrong installer, so make sure you choose the correct one based on your operating system and its version. Once the installation is complete, fire up the program with the following command:

jupyter notebook

You will notice that the tool isn't opened inside an application window, but in your browser instead. The next step is to press the "New" button in order to tell Jupyter which version of Python you are using. Keep in mind that in this book the chosen version is Python 3. Next, you should see a blank window which is your environment and interface.

The first thing you will notice with this particular environment is that you aren't dealing with a typical text editor. Instead, the code is organized in cell blocks that are executed one cell at a time. This design gives you the advantage of testing and verifying your code one small block at a time. Furthermore, you will notice that you have an input where you type your code and an output where the result is displayed. Now, let's type something to see how it all works:

In: print ("I'm testing Jupyter!")

In order to execute this line of code you should click on the play button. You can find it beneath the Cell tab. The result of the code will be displayed inside the output cell, followed by a blank input cell where you can continue typing. You will also notice a small plus symbol which is used to create more cells.

Summary

In this chapter you learned what it takes to set up your work environment in order to get started. You learned step by step how to install Python and the various options you have. You explored the option of using a scientific distribution instead of a manual installation and you learned how to setup a virtual environment. Remember that if you are the type of person always worrying about messing up, especially when working with code and terminal instructions, then you should use a virtual environment and eliminate all of your fears and doubts with one swift blow.

Furthermore, you explored a number of Python libraries, packages, and extensions which make data science a much more approachable field. All of these tools are free to download and install and they offer you a great deal of benefits. Keep in mind that this book relies on some of these libraries for the practical implementations. For instance, Scikit-learn is used throughout the book because it contains all the algorithms we are going to use, as well as all of the datasets. This way all you need to do is type a command to import them, instead of manually downloading them and setting them up.

Chapter 2: Data Munging with Pandas

Now that you're set up with all the tools you need and with a clean environment, it's time to begin with the data science process known as data munging. Sometimes known as data wrangling, this step is one of the most important ones in the entire data science pipeline. The basic concept behind it is that you need to process a set of data in order to be able to use it together with another set of data, or to analyze it. Essentially, you will make enough changes to an original dataset in order to make it more useful for your specific goals. This is a pre-processing step.

In order to understand this idea better, imagine that you have a set of data on which you need to apply a classification algorithm. However, you realize that you can't perform this step just yet because the dataset is a combination of continuous and categorical variables. This means that you have to modify some of these variables to match the correct format. The challenge here is that you are dealing with raw data and you cannot analyze it just yet. First you need to clean the data with various data munging techniques and tools.

In most real world scenarios you will be dealing with a great deal of data that is raw and cannot be analyzed just yet, unlike the datasets used for study and practice. This is why you need to clean the data and it can actually take you a great deal of time. In fact, many data scientists spend more time preparing the data instead of coding or running various algorithms. So how do we prepare our data? One of the most popular methods includes using the Pandas library which is used for data analysis and manipulation, as mentioned earlier. The purpose of this library in this case is to allow you to analyze raw, real world data a lot faster.

Keep in mind that the purpose of data munging is to gather enough information in order to be able to detect the pattern within it. Furthermore, data needs to be accurate in order to be useful to a data scientist or analyst in order to cut down on the time and resources needed to come up with meaningful results. With that in mind, the first step you need to take involves acquiring the data. After all, without data you can't do anything. However, before you gain access to it you need to understand that all data items are different and are not created equally. You will often have issues recognizing authentic data with an identified source. The second step is about joining the data once it has been extracted from every source. At this stage, the data needs to be modified and then combined in order to proceed at a later time with the analysis. Finally, we have the last step that involves cleaning the data. This stage is the main one. You will need to modify the data in order to obtain a format you can use. You might also have to perform optional steps like correcting noisy data or bad data that can negatively influence the results.

As you can already see, this step is essential although tedious and time consuming. However, you sometimes cannot avoid it. You will have to make sure that you have relevant, up to data information that doesn't contain any null values in order to select only the data you are interested in for analysis. Fortunately, Python together with Pandas are some of the most powerful tools you can use to aid you in data munging.

The Process

As already mentioned, even if data science projects are unique, the workflow is generally the same. It all begins with the acquisition of data. You can gather data in many ways. You can extract it from a database, from images, from spreadsheets and any other digital source that holds information. This is your raw data, however. You cannot use it for a proper analysis because among all that data you also have missing information and corrupted data. You need to first bring order to chaos by using Python data structures to turn the raw information into an organized data set made out of properly formatted variables. This dataset is then processed with the help of various algorithms.

Next, you can examine your data in order to come up with an early observation that you will later test. You will obtain new variables by processing the ones you currently have and move up the data science pipeline with the various techniques such as graph analysis and reveal the most valuable variables. You will now be able to create the first data model, however, your testing phase will tell you that you will have to apply a number of corrections to your data and therefore return to the data munging processes to rework each step. Keep in mind that in most cases the output you expect will not reflect the real output that you will receive. Theory doesn't always lead you in the direction you expect and that is why you need to process a number of different scenario and test to see what works.

Importing Datasets

Before we can do anything we need the actual data. In order to import a dataset we are going to use Pandas to access tabular information from various databases or spreadsheets. Essentially, this tool will build a data structure in which each row of the tabular file will be indexed, while also separating the variables so that we can manipulate the data. With that being said, we will work in Jupyter and type the following command to import Pandas into our environment and access a CSV file:

In: import pandas as pd

iris_filename = 'datasets-ucl-iris.csv'

iris = pd.read_csv(iris_filename, sep=',', decimal='.', header=None,

names= ['sepal_length', 'sepal_width', 'petal_length', 'petal_width', 'target'])

(Source: The Iris Dataset https://scikitlearn.org/stable/auto_examples/datasets/plot_iris_dataset.html retrieved in October 2019)

As you can see, the first step of this process is to import the tool we are going to use. Whether you are going to use Pandas or Scikit-learn, it is not enough to just have it installed on your system. You need to import it into your project in order to have access to its functions and features. Next, we created a new file and named it, while also defining the character that will act as a separator and a decimal. In this example the new file will contain an open source dataset that has been used to teach new data scientists and machine learners for years. The dataset is called Iris and it contains 50 samples of three different species of Iris flowers. We also mentioned that we don't want to define a header because it is not needed in our example. What we did so far was create a new data item named iris, which is in fact a data frame when we discuss it in the context of working with Pandas. In this case a data frame is actually the same as a Python list or dictionary, but with a set of added features. Next, we want to explore what the data item contains by typing:

In: iris.head()

This is a simple instruction without any parameters. By default if we don't specify we are going to access the first five rows from the file. If you want more, then you simply need to mention the number of rows you want to access by typing it as an argument between the parentheses of the function. Next, we want to read the names of the columns to see what kind of information they contain:

In: iris.columns

Out: Index(['sepal_length', 'sepal_width', 'petal_length',

'petal_width', 'target'], dtype='object')

As you can see in the output, what we have for now is an index of each column name. The structure of the output looks like a list. Now, let's obtain the target column:

In: Y = iris['target']

Y

This is what you should see as the output.

Out:

0   Iris-setosa

1   Iris -setosa

2   Iris -setosa

3   Iris -setosa

...

149   Iris-virginica

Name: target, dtype: object

The "Y" in this result is a series typical of Pandas. What you should know is that it is nearly identical to an array, however, it is only unidirectional. Furthermore, you will notice that the index class is the same as the one for a dictionary. Next, we are going to make a request to extract the list of columns by using the index:

In: X = iris[['sepal_length', 'sepal_width']]

Now we have the data frame, which is a matrix instead of a unidimensional series. The reason why it is a matrix is that we asked to extract several columns at once and therefore we essentially obtained an array that is structured in columns and rows. Now let's also obtain all of the dimensions.

In: print (X.shape)

Out: (150, 2)

In: print (Y.shape)

Out: (150)

The result is now a tuple and we can analyze the size of the array in either dimension. These are the bare bones basics of manipulating a new dataset and performing some basic exploration. Let's move on to the next step and preprocess the data so that we can actually use it.

Data Preprocessing

Now that you know how to load a dataset, let's explore the procedures you need to take in order to preprocess all the information within it. First, we are going to assume that we need to perform a certain action on a number of rows. In order to use any function, we first need to setup a mask. Take note that in this case a mask is in fact a collection of Boolean values that determine the selected line. The practical example will clear up this notion, so let's get to it:

In: mask_feature = iris['sepal_length'] > 7.0

In: mask_feature

0   False

1   False

...

146	True
147	True
148	True
149	False

As you can see we have chosen only the lines which contain a sepal length value that is greater than seven. These observations are declared with a Boolean value. Next, we are going to apply a mask in order to modify the iris virginica target and create a new label for it:

In: mask_target = iris['target'] == 'Iris-virginica'

In: iris.loc[mask_target, 'target'] = 'MyLabel'

Wherever the old iris virginica label appeared it will now be replaced with "MyLabel" as the new label. Take note that for this operation we need to use the "loc" function in order to gain access to the data with the help of the indexes. Now let's take the next step and see the labels that are contained by the target column:

In: iris['target'].unique()

Out: array(['Iris-setosa', 'Iris-versicolor', 'New label'],   dtype=object)

Now let's group all of the columns together:

In: grouped_targets_mean = iris.groupby(['target']).mean()

grouped_targets_mean

Out:

In: grouped_targets_var = iris.groupby(['target']).var()

grouped_targets_var

With this step we have grouped the columns together by using the groupby function. Take note that this is similar to the "group by" command that you have in SQL. In the next input line we have also applied the mean function which of course calculates the mean value. Keep in mind that we can apply this method either to a single column or multiple columns at the same time. Furthermore, we can use the variance, count, or sum functions in order to gain different values. Take note that the end result you obtain is also a Pandas data frame, which means you can connect all of these operations together. In this example we are grouping all of our data observations by labels in order to be able to analyze the difference between all the values inside the groups. But what if we also have time series to deal with?

In case you aren't familiar with time series, you should know that they imply the analysis of a collection of data entries that appear in an order. This order is determined chronologically. In essence, you are dealing with a group of points that are distributed in time with an equal space dividing each one of them. You will frequently encounter time series because they are used in many fields, usually regarding statistical analysis. For instance, when you have to work with weather data you will find time series regarding the forecasting or the detection of sunspots.

The next challenge, however, is dealing with data entries that contain noise. Keep in mind that while these training datasets have been documented and processed for years, they tend to be very clean and in fact they require very little preprocessing and cleaning. However, in the real world, you will frequently deal with noisy data. In that case, the first thing we can do is use a rolling function, which looks like this:

In: smooth_time_series = pd.rolling_mean(time_series, 5)

For this process we are applying the mean function once more. Keep in mind that you don't necessarily have to use the mean. You can also go with the median value instead. In addition, you will notice that we request to only access five samples. Next, we are going to use the apply function to perform a number of operations on our columns and rows. This is a function that can be used for multiple purposes, so let's start by determining how many non-zero items we have per line:

In: iris.apply (np.count_nonzero, axis=1).head()

Out: 0   5

1   5

2   5

3   5

4   5

dtype: int64

Finally, the applymap function is then used to perform operations on the elements themselves. Let's say that we need to obtain the value of the length for every single string representation inside every cell:

In: iris.applymap (lambda el:len(str(el))).head()

In order to obtain these values, the cells are casted to a string and then we can determine the length.

Now that you have an idea about using Pandas for data preprocessing, let's also discuss the topic of data selection with the help of the same tool.

Data Selection

What do we mean when we are referring to data selection? Let's assume that you have a dataset with an index column which you need to access in order to modify it and work with it. For the sake of this example, we are going to presume that the index starts from 100, like so:

n,val1,val2,val3

100,10,10,C

101,10,20,C

102,10,30,B

103,10,40,B

104,10,50,A

As you can see, the first row is row number 0 and its index value is 100. Once you import the file, you will see an index column as usual, however, there's the possibility of changing it or using it by mistake. Therefore, it would be a good idea to split the column from the rest of the data in order to avoid making any mistakes when you are running low on coffee. We are going to use Pandas to select the column and break it apart from the rest:

In: dataset = pd.read_csv('a_selection_example_1.csv',

index_col=0) dataset

That's it! Now you can manipulate the values as usual, whether you select the values by index, column, or line locations. For instance, you can access the fourth value from the fifth line which in our example has an index value equal to 105. Here's how the selection looks:

In: dataset['val4'][105]

You might be tempted to consider this to be a matrix, however, it isn't, so make sure not to make the confusion. In addition, you should always determine the column you want to access before you specify the row. This way you won't make any mistakes when looking to gain access to a certain cell's value.

Preparing your data and learning some surface information about it can greatly help you along the line, so make sure to always dedicate some time for data munging and preprocessing. In the next chapter, we are going to continue going deeper in order to gain further insight about the data exploration and data science pipeline as a whole.

Summary

In this chapter you learned the most elementary steps you need to take before starting to explore and analyze the data. You learned about data munging, which involves the preparation of data and how to work with a real dataset. You imported a real dataset and performed a number of basic operations on it with the purpose of preparing it for analysis. Now you know how to find out some basic information about your data, and therefore have a much easier time exploring it further. Keep in mind that while these steps may feel boring, they will make your job far easier down the line. In addition, you will gain much better results if you pre-process and explore your data as much as possible before you start implementing various learning algorithms and techniques.

Chapter 3: The Data Science Pipeline

So far we have imported a dataset and performed a few preprocessing operations with a series of Pandas function. The next step is to dive into the data science workflow. Preprocessing is a useful step, however, it is only the beginning, or the pre-beginning in fact.

In this section we are going to go through a series of somewhat challenging phases, so make sure to research and read the documentation of every tool we are going to use. We are going to discuss certain aspects about data science, such as creating new data features, performing dimensionality reduction, running performance tests and much more. All of this can be challenging and even overwhelming to a beginner, so make sure to read up on everything line by line and continue practicing the operations.

Exploring Data

The first phase within the data science workflow is performing the exploratory analysis. You need to gain a more detailed understanding of the data you are going to work with. This implies learning about the dataset's features, the shape of the elements, and using everything in order to form your hypothesis so that you can continue with the next steps. In this section we are going to continue working with the Iris dataset because it is very beginner-friendly and you are already somewhat familiar with it. So start by importing the dataset once more and create a new file like you did in the previous section. Once you've performed that step we can start exploring and go where no aspiring data scientist has gone before. Puns aside, we are going to use the describe function first in order to learn a bit more about our dataset:

```
In: iris.describe()
```

Now you should have access to various features such as deviation, minimum and maximum values, and so on. We need to take this basic data and analyze it at a deeper level, so let's start by exploring a graphical representation of it. For now we are going to use the simple "boxplot" function to create the plot, and not bother with Matplotlib just yet.

```
In: boxes = iris.boxplot(return_type='axes')
```

Keep in mind that you don't have to perform this step. Visualization is actually optional, unless you have to present your findings to someone who isn't very mathematically inclined but he or she can understand charts and plots much easier. For the same reason, as a beginner you should visualize your data so that you can place your focus elsewhere. Now, let's observe the relation between our features. For this step we are going to use a similarity matrix like this:

```
In: pd.crosstab(iris['petal_length'] > 3.758667, iris['petal_width'] > 1.198667)
```

You will notice that we are simply calculating the number of times the petal length appears when compared to the petal width. We are making this comparison with the crosstab function. If you look at the results you will see these features are well-related to each other. You can observe this even better by creating a scatterplot like so:

In: scatterplot = iris.plot(kind='scatter', x='petal_width',

y='petal_length', s=64, c='blue', edgecolors='white')

The scatterplot makes it easy to see that the petal width is connected to the length. When exploring data this way you can also use a different kind of graph, namely a histogram. In our case we are going to use one in order to see a display of the distribution of the values.

In: distr = iris.petal_width.plot(kind='hist', alpha=0.5, bins=20)

In this case we have selected twenty bins. If you aren't familiar with histograms you should know that bins refer to a variable's intervals. This is calculated by determining the square root of the total count of observations. That value represents the total number of bins.

New Features

Unfortunately, we are rarely so lucky to discover a close connection between certain features like we did in our basic example. That's when we need to apply a series of transformations. Let's say that you are trying to determine the value of a house. All you know for certain is the size of each room. You can use this information to create a new feature that represents the construction's volume. This transformation needs to be applied because we cannot observe the volume, however, we can observe features like length, width and height and then use these features to calculate the volume. Here's how all of this can be applied with code:

In: import numpy as np

from sklearn import datasets

from sklearn.cross_validation import train_test_split

from sklearn.metrics import mean_squared_error

cali = datasets.california_housing.fetch_california_housing()

X = cali['data']

Y = cali['target']

```
X_train, X_test, Y_train, Y_test = train_test_split(X, Y, train_size=0.8)
```

(Source: California Housing dataset

https://scikitlearn.org/stable/modules/generated/sklearn.datasets.fetch_california_housing.html retrieved in October 2019)

This time we imported a new dataset called California housing, which contains a great deal of data on the Californian housing market. In this example we are going to implement a regressor together with a mean absolute error with a value of 1.1575. If the code is difficult to understand and you don't know what a regressor is, don't worry about it at this time, we will discuss this later. All you need to understand for now is the concept we're discussing.

```
In: from sklearn.neighbors import KNeighborsRegressor

regressor = KNeighborsRegressor()

regressor.fit(X_train, Y_train)

Y_est = regressor.predict(X_test)

print ("MAE=", mean_squared_error(Y_test, Y_est))
```

Out: MAE= 1.15752795578

Now we need to try and reduce the value of the mean absolute error by implementing Z scores. This way we can perform the regression comparison and feature normalization. This process is also known as Z normalization because it seeks to map all of the original features to the new features we created. Let's continue:

```
In: from sklearn.preprocessing import StandardScaler

scaler = StandardScaler()

X_train_scaled = scaler.fit_transform(X_train)

X_test_scaled = scaler.transform(X_test)

regressor = KNeighborsRegressor()

regressor.fit(X_train_scaled, Y_train)

Y_est = regressor.predict(X_test_scaled)

print ("MAE=", mean_squared_error(Y_test, Y_est))
```

Out: MAE= 0.432334179429

The value of the mean absolute error has now been reduced from the previous value of approximately 1.15 to nearly 0.4, which is quite a great result. There are other methods that can be employed in order to minimize this value, however, the transformations required would be too complicated to implement at this state. What you should gain from this example is the fact that basic transformations can be easily applied and they can make your exploratory analysis much easier to conduct.

Dimensionality Reduction

In the real world you will often work with datasets that contain tens of thousands of data items, if not hundreds of thousands. Such datasets tend to also contain a large number of features, which means there will be some of them that you will not need. Just because the information exists, that doesn't mean it's useful. In some cases features are simply irrelevant and they just contribute to the noise. Noise is one of the elements which reduce the accuracy of your analysis and anything you can do to reduce it translates to an accuracy boost. When noise is caused by irrelevant features, your best option is to use dimensionality reduction methods.

As the name suggests, dimensionality reduction is all about reducing useless features and cutting back on the time it takes to process your data. In this section we are going to discuss a couple of techniques and algorithms you can use to eliminate the features you don't need.

Covariance Matrix

As mentioned earlier, you need to compare all of your features, or collections of features, in order to determine whether a relationship exists between them. You don't want to eliminate useful features. The covariance matrix is one of the techniques you'll be using to achieve this.

Dimensionality reduction implies the detection of relevant features, as well as the removal of the rest. Once you detect the ones that don't offer much, you can eliminate them. To demonstrate this concept, we are going to once again import the Iris dataset. Remember that this dataset contains four features for each observation, therefore a correlation matrix will yield some useful results.

In: from sklearn import datasets

import numpy as np

iris = datasets.load_iris()

cov_data = np.corrcoef(iris.data.T)

print (iris.feature_names)

print (cov_data)

And this is how your output should look as a result.

['sepal length (cm)', 'sepal width (cm)', 'petal length (cm)',

'petal width (cm)']

[[1. -0.10936925 0.87175416 0.81795363]

[-0.10936925 1. -0.4205161 -0.35654409]

[0.87175416 -0.4205161 1. 0.9627571]

[0.81795363 -0.35654409 0.9627571 1.]]

With the covariance matrix in place, let's create a visual representation of our results in order to have an easier time drawing conclusions. As a beginner, you should always use visualization methods because they are so much easier to read than pure numbers. This time we are going to import Matplotlib to draw the plot for us:

```
In: import matplotlib.pyplot as plt

img = plt.matshow(cov_data, cmap=plt.cm.rainbow)

plt.colorbar(img, ticks=[-1, 0, 1], fraction=0.045)

for x in range(cov_data.shape[0]):

for y in range(cov_data.shape[1]):

plt.text(x, y, "%0.2f" % cov_data[x,y],

size=12, color='black', ha="center", va="center")

plt.show()
```

You will notice that this time we haven't used a scatterplot or a histogram. In fact, we created a heat map. Take note of the most important value, which is 1. Every feature covariance has been normalized to a value of one in order to help us see the powerful connection between a number of features. By analyzing the heat map, you will notice that feature one has a strong relation to feature three, as well as four. The third feature is also strongly connected to the fourth feature. Finally, we have feature two which seems to have no relation to any of the other features. It is completely independent. Now that you know which features are useful and which one is irrelevant, you can cut some of the useless information.

Principal Component Analysis

The next step is to use an algorithm like the principal component analysis in order to define smaller features from their parent features. The new ones will be linear, however. This means that the output's first factor will have most of the variance. The second vector will have the most of the left over variance, and so on. The information will be aggregated to a new set of vectors that are formed after employing a principal component analysis.

The implementation relies on the fact that the vectors contain the data that comes from the input, and everything else is just noise. All you need to do in this case is to decide the number of vectors to have. The decision is made based on the variance, however. Let's take a look at the practical approach to this algorithm:

```
In: from sklearn.decomposition import PCA

pca_2c = PCA(n_components=2)

X_pca_2c = pca_2c.fit_transform(iris.data)

X_pca_2c.shape

Out: (150, 2)

In: plt.scatter(X_pca_2c[:,0], X_pca_2c[:,1], c = iris.target,

alpha=0.8, s=60, marker='o', edgecolors='white')

plt.show()

pca_2c.explained_variance_ratio_.sum()

Out:

0.97763177502480336
```

(Adapted from: https://educationalresearchtechniques.com/2018/10/24/factor-analysis-in-python/)

After the implementation, you will see that we only have two features in our output. The principal component analysis object is represented by the "n_components" object and its value is equal to two, which translates to what we just discussed.

We aren't going to dig deeper into the principal component analysis algorithm because it would just add an additional layer of confusion. For now, as a beginner, you should understand the concept of dimensionality reduction and not the inner workings of the algorithm. However, if you wish, you are encouraged to explore further. For now, we are going to move on to discussing another dimensionality reduction technique, namely the latent factor analysis.

Latent Factor Analysis

This concept is similar to the principal component analysis. The main idea here is that a latent factor always exists somewhere. Take note that a latent factor is just a variable, which cannot be observed through direct methods. We can only assume that our features are affected by a latent variable. This type of variable contains a specific kind of noise known as an arbitrary waveform generator. With that being said, let's see how this methodology is used for dimensionality reduction.

```
In: from sklearn.decomposition import FactorAnalysis

fact_2c = FactorAnalysis(n_components=2)

X_factor = fact_2c.fit_transform(iris.data)

plt.scatter(X_factor[:,0], X_factor[:,1], c=iris.target,

alpha=0.8, s=60, marker='o', edgecolors='white')

plt.show()
```

(Adapted from: https://educationalresearchtechniques.com/2018/10/24/factor-analysis-in-python/)

The difference in this case is that we establish the covariance between the variables in the output.

Outlier Detection

This next stage is one of the most important ones. Determining outliers is important because if we have any kind of erroneous information in our dataset, or partially incomplete data, adapting any new data will be extremely problematic. In turn, this issue can lead to algorithms that process faulty data and create inaccurate results.

So what is an outlier in this case? When we detect that a data point deviated from other data points we can compare them and establish that it is in fact an outlier. Let's discuss several cases where we have a different outlier in order to gain a better understanding of how to detect them and treat them.

Mainly there are three situations and each one is handled differently. Firstly, we will presume that the outlier is an infrequent appearance in whatever dataset we are working with. In this scenario, the information is based on another set of data from which it was extracted. Here we have a data sample which contains an outlier that is flagged as one because of its assumed rarity. This type of outlier is dealt with through a basic removal process.

In the second example, we have an outlier that frequently manifests itself. In this case it appears frequently. Whenever you experience similar occurrences, there's a sizable chance of encountering an error that affects the data sample generation. The problem here is that the algorithm's priority isn't the generalization, instead it focuses on learning the non-focused distribution. The outlier has to be eliminated.

The third situation involves a data point which is easy to conclude that it is in fact an error. Datasets often contain faulty data entries and they can easily cause inconsistencies in your data whenever you modify or manipulate the value. All you need to do in this case is delete the value and instruct the model to presume that it is a random loss. Another option is calculating and using an average value instead of the erroneous one. This is a preferable solution, however, if you find it difficult to implement it then simply delete the outlier.

Knowing these scenarios will help you understand which one you are experiencing, thus allowing you to have an easier time detecting the outlier and removing it. The first phase is to determine every single outlier and locate it. You can use two techniques to do this, though they are similar. You can either examine all separated variables individually, or all of them at once. These techniques are called the univariate and multivariate analysis.

You already had a brief introduction to the univariate method because you already worked with it unknowingly. If you recall, you created a graphical representation using a boxplot earlier. When this technique is used, you can determine which variable is in fact an outlier because you will see them as extremes. For instance, let's say you are observing the data description. If this observation is beneath the 25% ration or greater than 75%, you are probably looking at an outlier which can easily be seen in a box plot. The same applies if you are making Z-score observations, except in this case you are looking for a value above three. This method is one of the most efficient at detecting outliers, however, not all of them can be exposed with just one technique. This way you will only identify the extreme variables and others will escape undetected. In this case you should also consider the multivariate option, however, for now it's enough to stick to the basics and eliminate the most obvious outliers.

Summary

In this chapter you learned how to prepare your data for analysis and how to explore it. Once you imported your dataset you need to go through a series of preparation techniques in order to increase your chances of reaching an accurate result. Data exploration is crucial to the preparation of data, as well as various techniques such as dimensionality reduction. Furthermore, you learned how to apply these dimensionality reduction techniques in practice by implementing a covariance matrix and a principal component analysis algorithm.

In addition, you also learned about the importance of finding outliers within your data. Depending on the type of outliers and the learning algorithms you are using, they can severely impact the training process and the accuracy of the final result. In this chapter you learned about situations where they occur and why they should be eliminated.

Chapter 4: Supervised Learning Algorithms

Now that you understand the fundamentals of data preparation and manipulation we can start with the main course.

The algorithms used in data science can be divided into several categories, mainly supervised learning, unsupervised learning, and to some degree semi-supervised learning.

As the name suggests, supervised learning is aided by human interaction as the data scientist is required to provide the input and output in order to obtain a result from the predictions that are performed during the training process. Once the training is complete, the algorithm will use what it learned to apply on new, but similar data.

The idea of supervised learning can be compared to the way humans learn. As a student you are guided by a professor with examples. You work through those examples with his or her help until you are finally able to work on your own.

In this chapter we are going to focus on this type of learning algorithm. However, take note that their purpose is divided based on the problems they need to solve. Mainly there are two distinct categories, namely regression and classification. In the case of regression problems, your target is a numeric value, while in classification it is a class or a label. To make things clearer, an example of a regression task is determining the average value of houses in a given city. A classification task, on the other hand, is supposed to take certain data like the petal and sepal length, and based on that information determine which is the species of a flower.

With that in mind, let's start the chapter by discussing regression algorithms and how to work with them.

Regression

In data science, many tasks are resolved with the help of regression techniques. However, regression can also be categorized in two different branches, which are linear regression and logistic regression. Each one of them is used to solve different problems, however both of them are a perfect choice for prediction analyses because of the high accuracy of the results.

The purpose of linear regression is to shape a prediction value out of a set of unrelated variables. This means that if you need to discover the relation between a number of variables you can apply a linear regression algorithm to do the work for you. However, this isn't its main use. Linear regression algorithms are used for regression tasks. Keep in mind that logistic regression is not used to solve regression problems like the name suggests. Instead, it is used for classification tasks.

With that being said, we are going to start by implementing a linear regression algorithm on the Boston housing dataset, which is freely available and even included in the Scikit-learn library. This dataset contains 506 samples, with 13 features and a numerical type target. Unlike in our previous examples, this time the dataset will not be used as a whole. We are going to break it into two sections, a training and a testing set. There are no rules set in stone regarding the ratio of the split, however, it is generally accepted that it is best to keep the training set with a 70%-80% data distribution, and then save 20%-30% for the testing process.

Linear Regression

For this example we are going to use the Scikit-learn library because it contains the Boston dataset, therefore you don't have to download anything. Let's start the process by importing the dataset and splitting our data into two sets:

In: from sklearn.datasets import load_boston

boston = load_boston()

from sklearn.cross_validation import train_test_split

X_train, X_test, Y_train, Y_test = train_test_split(boston.data,

boston.target, test_size=0.2, random_state=0)

Pay attention to the train_test_split function because it is used to split the dataset into a training and a testing set. Keep in mind that it is also part of the Scikit-learn library, another reason why we are using this amazing tool. Furthermore, you will notice that the data is not randomly categorized. We need to specify certain parameters. In this case, by declaring the size of the test set to be equal to a value of 0.2 we also automatically declare that the training set should be 80% of the total data. You don't have to declare both parameters. In addition, we also have a random state parameter. Its purpose is to generate random numbers during the split.

Now, let's add in the regressor in order to predict the target value of the testing set. In addition, we will also measure the resulting accuracy and make sure there isn't too much noise influencing the result in a negative way.

In: from sklearn.linear_model import LinearRegression

regression = LinearRegression()

regression.fit(X_train, Y_train)

```
Y_pred = regression.predict(X_test)

from sklearn.metrics import mean_absolute_error

print ("MAE", mean_absolute_error(Y_test, Y_pred))
```

Out: MAE 3.82230762633

That's it! The result isn't the best and improvements can certainly be made. However, the purpose of this demonstration is to get you started with linear regression. For now you should focus on correct implementation. As you progress, you will learn more about optimization and fine tuning. Furthermore, you will also see that these algorithms involve two important factors, namely processing speed and prediction accuracy. Your choice is determining the balance between the two.

Logistic Regression

We will not focus on logistic regression in this chapter, however, you should understand what makes it different from linear regression and what defines it. The most important aspect you should always keep in mind is that there is no regressor involved, therefore it is usually implemented to solve classification problems, specifically those of a binary nature. Binary classification refers to performing a classification task when you only have two classes, in other words Boolean labels. The main goal of the Booleans labels is to offer us a true or false result so that we can conclude whether a result has been predicted or not.

Logistic regression may not be quite as popular as its regression solving brother, however, it has started being applied more and more in the medical field nowadays. However, a more popular method of solving binary classification problems is with the use of a Naive Bayse classifier, which we are going to discuss in the next section.

Naive Bayes Classifier

As mentioned, a popular algorithm for classification tasks is the Naive Bayes classifier. Take note that this algorithm can also be used to solve multiclass classification problems as well.

This classifier is a fairly old one, before data science entered the mainstream and everyone talked about Python. However, this doesn't mean that it's obsolete and no longer in use. On the contrary, it is highly popular when performing the categorization of textual information. In plain English, this means that the algorithm can process a number of documents and then categorize them appropriately based on the content. For instance, the classifier can determine which emails belong in your spam box. In other cases, this algorithm is also used in combination with support vector machines (we will discuss this soon) in order to process massive amounts of data with a greater efficiency.

There are three types of classifiers and you will use each one of them under certain circumstances. The first one is known as the Gaussian Naive Bayes, which is an algorithm that automatically presumes which features have a normal distribution and how they are related to each class. The second one is the Multinomial classifier, which is the most popular one when working with model events. This is the algorithm that is used to classify documents based on how often a certain term is found within the content. Lastly we have the Bernoulli classifier, which describes the inputs with binary variables. This algorithm is used for the same purpose as the multinomial classifier.

For the purpose of this beginner's guide to data science, we are not going to apply all three of these algorithms, however, you are free to use the knowledge you gathered so far to use the right tools and put them in application. In this section you will go through the demonstration on how to implement the Gaussian algorithm. This classifier is used more frequently than the other, therefore we will make it a priority.

To demonstrate the application we are going to use the Iris dataset once again:

```
In: from sklearn import datasets

iris = datasets.load_iris()

from sklearn.cross_validation import train_test_split

X_train, X_test, Y_train, Y_test = train_test_split(iris.data,

iris.target, test_size=0.2, random_state=0)

In: from sklearn.naive_bayes import GaussianNB

clf = GaussianNB()

clf.fit(X_train, Y_train)

Y_pred = clf.predict(X_test)
```

Just like before, we have divided the dataset into a training set and a testing set with an 80 by 20 division ratio. Then we imported the actual implementation of the algorithm from the Scikit-learn library in order to perform the classification task. The final step is acquiring the classification report so that we can see the data and form our own conclusions. Here's how a typical classification report looks:

```
In: from sklearn.metrics import classification_report

print (classification_report(Y_test, Y_pred))
```

Out:

	precision	recall	f1-score	support
0	1.00	1.00	1.00	12
1	0.93	1.00	0.96	11
2	1.00	0.83	0.91	7
avg / total	0.97	0.97	0.97	35

Take note of the four different metrics we have in the report. The first one is the precision metric which shows us the number of labels that are relevant. Next, we have the recall measure that gives us a value which represents the comparison between the relevant results and the labels. The third metric is the f1-score. This one is only important if we are dealing with a dataset that isn't well-balanced. The final metric we are interested in is the support measure that determines how many samples a certain class contains. In conclusion, the results we obtain after implementing the classifier are quite good. Now let's move to an even more powerful classifier that is used to solve complex problems.

K-Nearest Neighbors

This algorithm is one of the easiest ones to work with, however, it can solve some of the most challenging classification problems. The k-nearest neighbor algorithm can be used in various scenarios that require anything from compressing data to processing financial data. It is one of the most commonly used supervised machine learning algorithms and you should do your best to practice your implementation technique.

The basic idea behind the algorithm is the fact that you should explore relation between two different training observations. For instance, we will call them x and y, and if you have the input value of x, you can already predict the value of y. The way this works is by calculating the distance of a data point in relation to other data points. The k-nearest point is selected based on this distance and then it is assigned to a specific class.

To demonstrate how to implement this algorithm we are going to work with a much larger dataset than before, however, we will not use everything in it. Once again, we are going to rely on the Scikit-learn library in order to gain access to a dataset known as the MNIST handwritten digits dataset. This is in fact a database that holds roughly 70,000 images of handwritten digits which are distributed in a training set with 60,000 images and a test set with 10,000 images. However, as already mentioned, we are not going to use the entire dataset because that would take too long for this demonstration. Instead we will limit ourselves to 1000 samples. Let's get started:

```
In: from sklearn.utils import shuffle

from sklearn.datasets import

from sklearn.cross_validation import train_test_split

import pickle

mnist = pickle.load(open( "mnist.pickle", "rb" ))

mnist.data, mnist.target = shuffle(mnist.data, mnist.target)
```

As usual, we first import the dataset and the tools we need. However, you will notice one additional step here, namely object serialization. This means we converted an object to a different format so that it can be used later but also reverted back to its original version if needed. This process is referred to as pickling and that is why we have the seemingly out of place pickle module imported. This will allow us to communicate objects through a network if needed. Now, let's cut through the dataset until we have only 1000 samples:

```
mnist.data = mnist.data[:1000]

mnist.target = mnist.target[:1000]

X_train, X_test, y_train, y_test = train_test_split(mnist.data,

mnist.target, test_size=0.8, random_state=0)

In: from sklearn.neighbors import KNeighborsClassifier

# KNN: K=10, default measure of Euclidean distance

clf = KNeighborsClassifier(3)

clf.fit(X_train, y_train)

y_pred = clf.predict(X_test)
```

Now let's see the report with the accuracy metrics like earlier:

```
In: from sklearn.metrics import classification_report

print (classification_report(y_test, y_pred))
```

And here are the results:

Out:

	precision	recall	f1-score	support
0.0	0.68	0.90	0.78	79
1.0	0.66	1.00	0.79	95
2.0	0.83	0.50	0.62	76
3.0	0.59	0.64	0.61	85
4.0	0.65	0.56	0.60	75
5.0	0.76	0.55	0.64	80
6.0	0.89	0.69	0.77	70
7.0	0.76	0.83	0.79	76
8.0	0.91	0.56	0.69	77
9.0	0.61	0.75	0.67	87
avg / total	0.73	0.70	0.70	800

The results aren't the best, however, we have only implemented the "raw" algorithm without performing any kind of preparation operations that would clean and denoise the data. Fortunately the training speed was excellent even at this basic level. Remember, when working with supervised algorithms or any algorithms for that matter, you are always trading accuracy for processing speed or vice versa.

Support Vector Machines

The SVM is one of the most popular supervised learning algorithms due its capability of solving both regression as well as classification problems. In addition, it has the ability to identify outliers as well. This is one all-inclusive data science algorithm that you cannot miss. So what's so special about this algorithm?

First of all, support vector machines don't need much processing power in order to keep up with the prediction accuracy. We discussed several times how you are always dealing with a balancing act between accuracy and speed. This algorithm, however, is in a league of its own and you won't have to worry too much about sacrificing training speed for accuracy or the other way around. Furthermore, support vector machines can be used to eliminate some of the noise as well while performing the regression or classification tasks.

This type of algorithm has many real world applications and that is why it is important for you to understand its implementation. It is used in facial recognition software, text classification, handwriting recognition software and so on. The basic concept behind it, however, simply involves the distance between the nearest points where a hyperplane is selected from the margin between a number of support vectors. Take note that what is known as a hyperplane here is the object that divides the information space for the purpose of classification.

To put all of this theory in application we are going to rely on the Scikit-learn library once again. The algorithm will be implemented in such a way to demonstrate the accuracy of the prediction in the case of identifying real banknotes. We mentioned earlier that support vector machines are effective when it comes to image classification, therefore this algorithm is perfectly suited for our goals. What we need to solve in this example is a simple binary classification problem because we need to train the algorithm to determine whether the banknote is valid or not.

The bill will be described using several attributes. Keep in mind that unlike the other classification algorithms, a support vector machine determines its decision limit by defining the maximum distance between the data points which are nearest to the relevant classes. However, we aren't looking to limit the decision, we just want to find the best one. The nearest points in this best decision are what we refer to as support vectors. With that being said, let's import a new dataset and several tools:

import numpy as np

import pandas as pd

```
import matplotlib.pyplot as plt

dataset = pd.read_csv ("bank_note.csv")
```

As usual, the first step is learning more about the data we are working with. Let's learn how many rows and columns we have and then obtain the data from the first five rows only:

```
print (dataset.shape)

print (dataset.head())
```

Here's the result:

	Variance	Skewness	Curtosis	Entropy	Class
0	3.621600	8.6661	-2.8073	-0.44699	
1	4.454590	8.1674	-2.4586	-1.46210	0
2	3.86600	-2.6383	1.9242	0.10645	0
3	3.456600	9.5228	-4.0112	-3.59440	-
4	0.32924	-4.4552	4.5718	-0.98880	0

(Source: Based on https://archive.ics.uci.edu/ml/datasets/banknote+authentication retrieved in October 2019)

Now we need to process this information in order to establish the training and testing sets. This means that we need to reduce the data to attributes and labels only:

```
x = dataset.drop ('Class', axis = 1)

y = dataset ['Class']
```

The purpose of this code is to store the column data as the x variable and then apply the drop function in order to avoid the class column so that we can store it inside a 'y' variable. By reducing the dataset to a collection of attributes and labels we can start defining the training and testing data sets. Split the data just like we did in all the earlier examples. Next, let's start implementing the algorithm.

We need Scikit-learn for this step because it contains the support vector machine algorithm and therefore we can easily access it without requiring outside sources.

```
from sklearn.svm import SVC

svc_classifier = SVC (kernel = 'linear')

svc_classifier.fit (x_train, y_train)

pred_y = svc.classifier.predict(x_test)
```

Finally, we need to check the accuracy of our implementation. For this step we are going to use a confusion matrix which will act as a table that displays the accuracy values of the classification's performance. You will see a number of true positives, true negatives, as well as false positives and false negatives. The accuracy value is then determined from these values. With that being said, let's take a look at the confusion matrix and then print the classification report:

```
from sklearn.metric import confusion_matrix

print (confusion_matrix (y_test, pred_y)
```

This is the output:

```
[[160  1]

 [1       113]]
```

Accuracy Score: 0.99

Now let's see the familiar classification report:

```
from sklearn.metrics import classification_report

print (classification_report(y_test, y_pred))
```

And here are the results of the report:

	precision		recall	f1-score		support
0.0	0.99	0.99	0.99	161		
1.0		0.99	0.99	0.99	114	
avg / total		0.99	0.99	0.99	275	

Based on all of these metrics, we can determine that we obtained a very high accuracy with our implementation of the support vector machines. A score of 0.99 is almost as good as it can get, however, there is always room for improvement.

Summary

In this chapter we have focused on supervised learning algorithms and techniques. This category of learning techniques contains some of the most beginner-friendly algorithms and methods of exploring and analyzing data. The purpose of this chapter is to offer you a practical introduction to topics such as linear regression, K-nearest neighbors, support vector machines and much more. Each concept is discussed in detail because they will serve as the foundation for any aspiring data scientist and machine learner. Just make sure to go over the code for each algorithm and learning technique and study the tools that we are using for the implementation.

Chapter 5: Decision Trees

Decision trees are built similarly to support vector machines, meaning they are a category of supervised machine learning algorithms that are capable of solving both regression and classification problems. They are powerful and used when working with a great deal of data.

It is important for you to learn beyond the barebones basics so that you can process large and complex datasets. Furthermore, decision trees are used in creating random forests, which is arguably the most powerful learning algorithm. In this chapter we are going to exclusively focus on decision trees explicitly because of their popular use and efficiency.

Implementing Decision Trees

Decision trees are essentially a tool which supports a decision that will influence all the other decisions that will be made. This means that everything from the predicted outcomes to consequences and resource usage will be influenced in some way. Take note that decision trees are usually represented in a graph, which can be described as some kind of chart where the training tests appear as a node. For instance, the node can be the toss of a coin which can have two different results. Furthermore, branches sprout in order to individually represent the results and they also have leaves which are in fact the class labels. Now you see why this algorithm is called a decision tree. The structure resembles an actual tree. As you probably guessed, random forests are exactly what they sound like. They are collections of decision trees, but enough about them.

Decision trees are one of the most powerful supervised learning methods you can use, especially as a beginner. Unlike other more complex algorithms they are fairly easy to implement and they have a lot to offer. A decision tree can perform any common data science task and the results you obtain at the end of the training process are highly accurate. With that in mind, let's analyze a few other advantages, as well as disadvantages, in order to gain a better understanding of their use and implementation.

Let's begin with the positives:

1. Decision trees are simple in design and therefore easy to implement even if you are a beginner without a formal education in data science or machine learning. The concept behind this algorithm can be summarized with a sort of a formula that follows a common type of programming statement: If this, then that, else that. Furthermore, the results you will obtain are very easy to interpret, especially due to the graphic representation.

2. The second advantage is that a decision tree is one of the most efficient methods in exploring and determining the most important variables, as well as discovering the connection between then. In addition, you can build new features easily in order to gain better measurements and predictions.

Don't forget that data exploration is one of the most important stages in working with data, especially when there's a large number of variables involved. You need to be able to detect the most valuable ones in order to avoid a time consuming process, and decision trees excel at this.

3.   Another benefit of implementing decision trees is the fact that they are excellent at clearing up some of the outliers in your data. Don't forget that outliers are noise that reduces the accuracy of your predictions. In addition, decision trees aren't that strongly affected by noise. In many cases outliers have such a small impact on this algorithm that you can even choose to ignore them if you don't need to maximize the accuracy scores.

4.   Finally, there's the fact that decision trees can work with both numerical as well as categorical variables. Remember that some of the algorithms we already discussed can only be used with one data type or the other. Decision trees, on the other hand, are proven to be versatile and handle a much more varied set of tasks.

As you can see, decision trees are powerful, versatile, and easy to implement, so why should we ever bother using anything else? As usual, nothing is perfect, so let's discuss the negative side of working with this type of algorithm:

1.   One of the biggest issues encountered during a decision tree implementation is overfitting. Take note that this algorithm tends to sometimes create very complicated decision trees that will have issues generalizing data due to their own complexity. This is known as overfitting and it is encountered when implementing other learning algorithms as well, however, not to the same degree. Fortunately, this doesn't mean you should stay away from using decision trees. All you need to do is invest some time to implement certain parameter limitations to reduce the impact of overfitting.

2.   Decision trees can have issues with continuous variables. When continuous numerical variables are involved, the decision trees lose a certain amount of information. This problem occurs when the variables are categorized. If you aren't familiar with these variables, a continuous variable can be a value that is set to be within a range of numbers. For example, if people between ages 18 and 26 are considered of student age, then this numerical range becomes a continuous variable because it can hold any value between the declared minimum and maximum.

While there are some disadvantages that can add to additional work in the implementation of decision trees, the advantages still outweigh them by far.

Classification and Regression Trees

We discussed earlier that decision trees are used for both regression tasks as well as classification tasks. However, this doesn't mean you implement the exact same decision trees in both cases. Decision trees need to be divided into classification and regression trees. They handle different problems, however, they are similar in some ways since they are both types of decision trees.

Take note that classification decision trees are implemented when there's a categorical dependent variable. On the other side, a regression tree is only implemented in the case of a continuous dependent variable. Furthermore, in the case of classification tree, the result from the training data is in fact the mode of the total relevant observations. This means that any observations that we cannot define will be predicted based on this value, which represents the observation which we identify most frequently.

Regression trees on the other hand work slightly differently. The value that results from the training stage is not the mode value, but the mean of the total observations. This way the unidentified observations are declared with the mean value which results from the known observations.

Both types of decision trees undergo a binary split however, going from the top to bottom. This means that the observations in one area will spawn two branches that are then divided inside the predictor space. This is also known as a greedy approach because the learning algorithm is seeking the most relevant variable in the split while ignoring the future splits that could lead to the development of an even more powerful and accurate decision tree.

As you can see, there are some differences as well as similarities between the two. However, what you should note from all of this is that the splitting is what has the most effect on the accuracy scores of the decision tree implementation. Decision tree nodes are divided into subnodes, no matter the type of tree. This tree split is performed in order to lead to a more uniform set of nodes.

Now that you understand the fundamentals behind decision trees, let's dig a bit deeper into the problem of overfitting.

The Overfitting Problem

You learned earlier that overfitting is one of the main problems when working with decision trees and sometimes it can have a severe impact on the results. Decision trees can lead to a 100% accuracy score for the training set if we do not impose any limits. However, the major downside here is that overfitting creeps in when the algorithm seeks to eliminate the training errors, but by doing so it actually increases the testing errors. This imbalance, despite the score, leads to terrible prediction accuracy in the end result. Why does this happen? In this case the decision trees grow many branches and that's the cause of overfitting. In order to solve this use, you need to impose limitations to how much the decision tree can develop and how many branches it can spawn. Furthermore, you can also prune the tree to keep it under control, much like how you would do with a real tree in order to make sure it produces plenty of fruit.

In order to limit the size of the decision tree, you need to determine new parameters during the definition of the tree. Let's analyze these parameters:

1. min_samples_split: The first thing you can do is change this parameter to

specify how many observations a node will require in order to be able to perform the splitting. You can declare anything with a range of one sample to maximum samples. Just keep in mind that in order to limit the training model from determining the connections that are very common to a particular decision tree you need to increase the value. In other words, you can limit the decision tree with higher values.

2. min_samples_leaf: This is the parameter you need to tweak in order to determine how many observations are required by a node, or in other words a leaf. The overfitting control mechanism works the same way as for the samples split parameter.

3. max_features: Adjust this parameter in order to control the features that are selected randomly. These features are the ones that are used to perform the best split. In order to determine the most efficient value you should calculate the square root of the total features. Just keep in mind that in this case, the higher value tends to lead to the overfitting problem we are trying to fix. Therefore, you should experiment with the value you set. Furthermore, not all cases are the same. Sometimes a higher value will work without resulting in overfitting.

4. max_depth: Finally, we have the depth parameter which consists of the depth value of the decision tree. In order to limit the overfitting problem, however, we are only interested in the maximum depth value. Take note that a high value translates to a high number of splits, therefore a high amount of information. By tweaking this value you will have control over how the training model learns the connections in a sample.

Modifying these parameters is only one aspect of gaining control of our decision trees in order to reduce overfitting and boost performance and accuracy. The next step after applying these limits is to prune the trees.

Pruning

This technique might sound too silly to be real, however, it is a legitimate machine learning concept that is used to improve your decision tree by nearly eliminating the overfitting issue. As with real trees, what pruning does is reduce the size of the trees in order to focus the resources on providing highly accurate results. However, you should keep in mind that the segments that are pruned are not entirely randomly selected, which is a good thing. The sections that are eliminated are those that don't really help with the classification process and don't lead to any performance boosts. Less complex decision trees lead to a better optimized model.

In order to better understand the difference between an unmodified decision tree and one that was pruned and optimized, you should visualize the following scenario. Let's say that there's a highway that has a lane for vehicles that travel at 80 mph, and a second lane for the slower vehicles that travel at 50 mph. Now let's assume you are on this highway in a red car and you are facing a decision. You have the option to move on the fast lane in order to pass a slow moving car, however, this means that you will have a truck in front of you that can't achieve the high speed he should have in the left lane and therefore you will be stuck on that lane. In this case, the cars that are in the other lane are slowly starting to overpass you because the truck can't keep up. The other option is staying in your lane without attempting to make a pass. The most optimal choice here is the one that allows you to travel a longer distance during a certain amount of time. Therefore if you choose to stay in the slow lane until you gradually pass the truck that is blocking the fast lane, you will eventually be able to switch to that lane and pass all the other vehicles. As you can see, the second option might look slow at the time of consideration, however, in the long run it ends up being the most efficient one. Decision trees are the same. If you apply limits to your trees, they won't get greedy by switching you to the left lane where you will be stuck behind a truck. However, if you prune the decision tree, it will allow you to examine your surroundings in more detail and allow you predict a higher number of options you have in order to be able to make a better choice.

As you can see, performing the pruning process does yield a number of benefits which cannot be ignored. However, the implementation of this technique requires a number of steps and conditions. For instance, for a decision tree to be suitable for pruning, it needs to have a high depth value. Furthermore, the process needs to start at the bottom in order to avoid any negative returns. This issue needs to be avoided because if we have a negative node split at the bottom and another one occurs at the top, we will end up with a decision tree that will stop when the first division occurs. If the tree is pruned, it will not stop there and you will have higher gains.

Visualizing decision trees can sometimes be difficult when all you have is theory, so let's start with a step by step implementation to see them in action.

Decision Tree Implementation

Creating a decision tree starts from the root node. The first step is to select one of the data attributes and set up a logical test based on it. Once you have a set of results you can branch out and create another set of tests, which will you will use to create the subnode. Once we have at least a subnode we can apply a recursive splitting process on it in order to determine that we have clean decision tree leaves. Keep in mind that the level of purity is determined based on the number of cases that sprout from a single class. At this stage you can start pruning the tree in order to eliminate anything that doesn't improve the accuracy of the classification stage. Furthermore, you will also have to evaluate every single split that is performed based on each attribute. This step needs to be performed in order to determine which is the most optimal attribute, as well as split.

But enough theory for now. All you should focus on at this point is the fundamental idea behind decision trees and how to make them efficient. Once you think you grasped the basics, you need to start the implementation.

In the following example we will once again rely on the Iris dataset for the data, and the Scikit-learn library which contains it.

With that being said, let's continue with the practical implementation before the theory becomes too overwhelming. What's important at this stage is to understand the fundamental concepts and more importantly how to apply them in practice. With that being said, let's see what a decision tree looks like in code. Once again, we are going to use the Iris dataset, which is part of the Scikit-learn library. We will use other packages as well, such as Pandas and Numpy, so let's take a look at the code and discuss further:

```
%matplotlib inline
```

```
import pandas as pd
```

```
import numpy as np
```

```
import seaborn as sns
```

```
import matplotlib.pyplot as plt
```

```
from sklearn.model_selection import train_test_split
```

```
from sklearn.tree import DecisionTreeClassifier
```

```
df = pd.read_csv('Iris.csv')
```

Once all packages and modules are imported, we need to check the values to see if we have any null values:

```
df.isnull().any()
```

Take note that there are no null values in the dataset, however, this check should always be performed just to be certain. Always remember that data exploration is one of the most crucial steps and you should never avoid performing it. Make sure to perform all the other exploration steps we discussed earlier in the book in order to be as familiar with the data as possible. Once you consider you have analyzed and explored the data in enough detail, you can perform the analysis to determine the connection between the data columns. For this purpose in this example we are using the "seaborn" module because it contains the "pairplot" function, which will allow us to visualize all the connections. We will use a certain color for each column and then look for any outliers. Here's how to use this function:

```
sns.pairplot(df, hue = 'Species')
```

Take note that we do have a small number of outliers. In this case, they can probably be ignored because they are only a few and they most likely represent data anomalies and incorrect entries. For the purpose of this example we are going to assume they are nearly irrelevant anomalies and not pay them much attention.

The next step is performing the train / test split. Keep in mind that while in all other examples we have used a 80 / 20 ratio, this time we are going to have 30% of the data saved for the test set. Now let's take a look at the code:

```
all_inputs = df [['SepalLengthCm', 'SepalWidthCm', 'PetalLengthCm',
'PetalWidthCm']].values
```

```
all_classes = df ['Species'].values
```

```
(train_inputs, test_inputs, train_classes, test_classes) =
```

```
train_test_split (all_inputs, all_classes, train_size = 0.7, random_state = 1)
```

Notice that the random state is set to a value of one in order to make sure we always have an identical data split. This is not crucial for our decision tree example, however, if we ever want to recreate the dataset in the exact same way, we need this value.

Now, let's handle the classification process. We can now finally implement the decision tree:

```
dtc = DecisionTreeClassifier()
```

```
dtc.fit (train_inputs, train_classes)
```

```
dtc.score (test_inputs, test_classes)
```

The result should look something like this:

```
0.955
```

That's it! This is a simple example, but we already managed to achieve 95% accuracy. Now imagine if we would dedicate some time to polishing the decision tree as much as possible. This is why they are so frequently used to solve complex problems. Ultimately, they are easy to implement even if the theory makes it sound difficult, and they offer great results with minimal negative side effects.

Summary

In this chapter you explored decision trees and learned how they are implemented. You studied concepts such as backpropagation and pruning and you learned what advantages and disadvantages you will encounter when working with classification and regression trees. Remember that decision trees are powerful and very useful, however they sometimes need to be used together with other technique in order to enhance some of their characteristics. While they are easy to implement, you should study them in detail because they are often used in data science and Big Data, especially in the form of Random Forests. In this book we aren't going to expand on the concept of Random Forests, however, you should know that they are powerful and versatile in dealing with complex data because they are collections of decision trees. So, make sure you fully understand the concept of decision trees before progressing to more complex topics.

Chapter 6: Unsupervised Learning with K-means Clustering

Unlike supervised learning, this category of algorithms learns only from already established examples without human intervention. These algorithms are often used to process massive datasets that contain only inputs. Their objective is to identify the clusters of data points in order to compare them next to those coming from other datasets.

Unsupervised learning algorithms learn differently from supervised algorithms. They learn from unlabeled data, which hasn't been classified. They seek to define an output based on the common relations found in the inputs. That output is then applied to other datasets as well. Because of their learning mechanism, these algorithms are often used for tasks like explaining data features and statistical density estimations. Unsupervised learning can also be used anywhere where we need to discover what kind of anomalies the input data contains.

Unsupervised learning algorithms are mainly used to learn from complex datasets. Therefore, their top priority is performing an exploratory analysis and identifying important data. One such algorithm is known as the K-means Clustering algorithm and this chapter will focus on it alone. This learning technique is one of the most popular clustering algorithms that is used to discover predictable patterns in large datasets.

K-means Clustering

As mentioned, unsupervised learning methods are ideal for working with unlabeled data. However, to be more specific, one of the best techniques, if not the best, is to use a type of clustering algorithm. The main idea behind this approach is the cluster analysis which involves reducing data observations to clusters, or subdivisions of data, where each cluster contains information that is similar to that of a predefined attribute. Clustering involves a number of techniques that all achieve the same goal because they are all about forming a variety of theories regarding the data structure.

One of the most popular unsupervised learning algorithms and clustering techniques is known as k-means clustering. This concept revolves around building data clusters based on the similarity of the values. The first step is to determine the value of k, which is in fact represented by the total number of clusters we define. These clusters are built as k-many points, which hold the average value that represents the entire cluster. Furthermore, the values are assigned based on the value which is the closest average. Keep in mind that clusters have a core which is defined as an average value which pushes the other averages aside, changing them. After enough iterations, the core value will shift itself to a point where the performance metric is lower. When this stage is reached, we have the solutions because there aren't any observations available to be designated.

If you're confused by now by all this theory, that's ok. You will see that this technique is a lot easier than it sounds. Let's take a look at the practical implementation. In this example we will use the UCI handwritten digits dataset. It is freely available and you don't need to download if you are using Scikit-learn along with the book. With that being said, here's the code:

```python
from time import time

import numpy as np

import matplotlib.pyplot as plt

from sklearn import datasets

np.random.seed()

digits = datasets.load_digits()

data = scale(digits.data)

n_samples, n_features = data.shape

n_digits = len(np.unique(digits.target))

labels = digits.target

sample_size = 300

print("n_digits: %d, \t n_samples %d, \t n_features %d"

% (n_digits, n_samples, n_features))

print(79 * '_')

print('% 9s' % 'init"    time inertia homo compl v-meas

ARI      AMI silhouette')

def bench_k_means(estimator, name, data):

t0 = time()

estimator.fit(data)

print('% 9s %.2fs %i %.3f %.3f %.3f %.3f %.3f %.3f'

        % (name, (time() - t0), estimator.inertia_,
```

```
metrics.homogeneity_score(labels, estimator.labels_),

metrics.completeness_score(labels, estimator.labels_),

metrics.v_measure_score(labels, estimator.labels_),

metrics.adjusted_rand_score(labels, estimator.labels_),

metrics.silhouette_score(data, estimator.labels_,

        metric='euclidean',

        sample_size=sample_size)))
```

(Source: K Means clustering – Implementing k Means. Adapted from https://techwithtim.net/tutorials/machine-learning-python/k-means-2/ accessed in October 2019)

If you analyze the code line by line you will notice that the implementation is fairly simple, logical, and easy to understand. In fact, it is somewhat similar in parts to other techniques we used so far. However, there is one major difference that is important to mention, namely the performance measurements we are using in order to accurately interpret the data.

First we have a homogeneity score. This metric can have a value between zero and one. It mainly seeks the clusters that make room only for one class systems. The idea is that if we have a score that is close to the value of one, then the cluster is mostly built from the samples that belong to a single class. On the other hand, if the score is close to zero, then we have achieved a low homogeneity.

Next, we have the completeness score. This metric compliments the homogeneity measure. Its purpose is to give us information on how the measurements became part of a specific class. The two scores allow us to form the conclusion that we either managed to perform perfect clustering, or we simply failed.

The third metric is known as the V-metric, or sometimes the V-measure. This score is calculated as the harmonic mean of the previous two scores. The V-metric essentially checks on the homogeneity and the completeness score by assigning a zero to one value that verifies the validity.

Next, we have the adjusted Rand index metric. This is a score that is used to verify the similarity of the labeling. Using a value between zero and one, the Rand index simply determines the relation between the distribution sets.

Finally, we have the silhouette metric which is used to verify whether the performance of the clustering is sufficient without having labeled data. The measurement goes from a value of negative one to positive one and it determines whether the clusters are well-structured or not. If the number is anywhere close to negative one then we are dealing with bad clusters. In order to make sure we have dense clusters, we need to achieve a score close to positive one. Keep in mind that in this case we can also have a score that is close to zero. In this case the silhouette measurement tells us that we have clusters which are overlapping each other.

Now that you understand the measurement system, we have to apply one more step to this implementation and make sure that the results are accurate. To verify the clustering scores we can use the bench_k_means function like so:

```
bench_k_means(KMeans(init='k-means++', n_clusters=n_digits, n_ init=10),

name="k-means++", data=data) print(79 * '_')
```

Now let's see what conclusion we can draw from the scores. Here's how your results should look:

n_digits: 10,   n_samples 1797,   n_features 64

init	time	inertia	homo	compl
k-means++	0.25s	69517	0.596	0.643

init	v-meas	ARI	AMI	silhouette
k-means++	0.619	0.465	0.592	0.123

As you can see, with a basic k-means implementation we have fairly decent scores, however, there is a lot we could improve. Clustering is sufficient, but we could perfect the scores by implementing other supervised or unsupervised learning techniques. For instance, in this case you might consider using the principal component analysis algorithm as well. Another option would be applying various dimensionality reduction methods. However, for the purpose of learning how to implement the K-means clustering algorithm, these results will suffice. However, you should keep in mind that in the real world of data science you will often implement a number of algorithms and techniques together. You will almost never be able to get useful results with just one algorithm, especially when working with raw datasets instead of the practice ones.

Summary

In this chapter we have focused on learning about unsupervised learning algorithms, namely K-means clustering. The purpose of this section was to show you a technique that can be used on more complex datasets. Clustering algorithms are the staple of data science and frequently used, especially in combination with other algorithms and learning techniques. Furthermore, as you will learn later, clustering techniques, especially K-means clustering, are highly efficient in dealing with Big Data.

Chapter 7: Neural Networks

Artificial neural networks were designed theoretically in the 1950s, with the purpose of finding a way to copy the human thinking and decision making process. The idea was to create a learning system that would function similarly to the human brain. However, keep in mind that this didn't involve the attempt to replicate the human brain or neural network. What the artificial and the natural systems had in common is only the shallow resemblance. Artificial neural networks were created using the inspiration that came from exploring the human neural network.

Neural networks consist of neurons, or nodes to be more precise. These nodes are in fact just code which seeks to find the solution to a problem through repeated execution. Once an answer is found, it is communicated to the next node which in turn will process that information. These nodes are setup in a system of layers. In other words, there are separate layers that consist of a certain number of nodes and these layers are separate from each other, though they do communicate. First the communication is done only through the nodes of the same layer and only then the information is passed on to the following layer. Based on this simple description, you can already determine that the artificial neural network is nowhere near the human neural net when it comes to capability and processing power. Data travels in a somewhat linear fashion, from node to node and layer to layer. Human processing however is parallel, which means that the data is processed at the same time throughout the vast interconnected network of neurons.

Now that you understand the basic concept behind a neural network we can dive into this chapter and discuss its design and the various types of neural networks that we can implement.

Neural Network Structures

So far you learned that when in a neural network data is explored, classified and then pushed to the next node, ultimately traveling through the whole network. We also mentioned layers, however, take note that there are three different categories of layers. First we have the input layer and the output layer. Between these layers however, we have what is known as a hidden layer. This is where the input layer sends all of the data it analyzes. Keep in mind that neural networks can also function without the hidden layer and only use the two basic input and output layers. On the other end of the spectrum we can also develop networks with hundreds of layers. In this chapter we are going to focus on the more classic design which is based on having the three layers. Generally speaking, if a neural network consists of more than these layers it turns into a deep learning system. This type of network is different and as a beginner there's no need to get into it just yet.

As you may have guessed already, the structure of neural networks is influenced by the way the nodes are arranged inside the network. With each arrangement we end up with a different neural network. The most common arrangements lead to the development of the feedforward neural networks, recurrent neural networks and the Boltzmann machine, just to list a few. Each one of these networks has a different structure and serves a different purpose.

Now let's discuss the structure of a basic network in more detail.

As already discussed, a common network has three layers, but not always. For instance, without any hidden layers, we start working with logistic regression. The input layer is designed to contain an observation matrix that has five units. The output layer, however, has three units. In the case of the output, we need to determine the difference between the three units, or classes, and therefore we have to classify them. In the case of the input, we are dealing with constrained numerical features which need to be turned into categorical features. The hidden layer on the other hand starts with eight units, but this is only the minimum value. There is no actual limitation to how many units there can be, and as already mentioned, there is no limit to the amount of hidden layers we have either. Due the lack of restrictions in this case, the data scientist needs to use his best judgment to make the right decision regarding the type of network he or she implements.

With the fundamentals fresh in your mind, let's discuss the first neural network model, which is the feedforward neural net.

The Feedforward Neural Network

This is the fundamental design of the neural network as it consists of the three basic elements that communicate in a line. The input layer sends data to the hidden layer, which in turn sends it to the output layer. Take note that this type of neural network does not seek to iterate. In other words, the data inside the input layer is processed and the result can be found only in the output layer. In addition, there are two categories of feedforward networks, namely the single layer perceptron and the multilayer perceptron.

The simplest type of neural network you can have is the single layer perceptron. This is a type of feedforward neural network that contains only one node per layer. The node has an input that is directly connected to the node of the next layer because there are no other nodes around it. The second node, however, is in fact the weighted sum of the inputs. The input data is defined by the node and if a certain condition is met, then we gain a result. The single layer perceptron is used only to classify the data into two different parts, therefore it is also known as a linear binary classifier.

Another simplistic neural network is the multilayer perceptron. In this case we have to have at least two layers, however, in a real world implementation we would have quite a few more. The main difference between this model and the single layer perceptron, however, is the fact that the output of one layer turns into the input of the following layer. This architecture is based on a concept called backpropagation (more on this soon). With this design we have to perform a comparison check between the output we assume and the real output. In the event that we find a high inaccuracy level, the data is transmitted once again through the entire network. During the second round of processing the node's weights will be adjusted in order to improve the accuracy level. Keep in mind that this process repeats itself multiple times until the result is accurate. While the single layer perceptron has limited use, as the first type of neural network ever devised, the multilayer perceptron has a wide range of usability because of this efficient structure.

Next up we have the recurrent neural network structures, however before moving on to that topic we should clear up what the concept of backpropagation involves.

Backpropagation

Backpropagation is a concept that appeared in the 70s when neural networks were mostly theoretical. Back then computers were simply not powerful and efficient enough to handle an artificial neural network, therefore, even though this technological advancement was already designed, it could not be applied. Even today working with a neural network requires a great deal of resources from your computer. But let's leave history in the past and see what backpropagation is all about.

This concept is in fact a mathematical concept and therefore we will not dig deep into the subject because we are only interested in the theory and what it means to you as an aspiring data scientist.

Remember that there is always a difference between the imagined output and the actual output. Furthermore, you should focus on the fact that each node has a weight assigned to it, which is adjusted based on the information that arrives from the input. The purpose of backpropagation is to find the off-shoot of this mathematical difference between the two outputs. This result is then applied to the next iteration in order to give the nodes the ability to adjust their weights. This is why every single time the data is processed through the entire network, the inaccuracy level is reduced.

Just in case you are having difficulty with this theory, you should imagine the following scenario. Let's say that you are out playing basketball. You throw the ball to score, but unfortunately it just hits the hoop itself and by doing so the ball just starts going around the ring. With every single pass, the ball will slow down and fall slightly inwards towards the center of the hoop. Eventually, after enough passes the ball will go down through the ring. This is how backpropagation can also be visualized. Every loop the ball completes is in fact an iteration. The more iterations we have, the closer we get to the result, or in our case, the closer the ball gets to the center of the ring. With each pass, the output becomes closer to what we expect.

In data science one of the main goals is to process data automatically with supervised and unsupervised machine learning methods. This same goal applied to artificial neural networks. There is one notable difference, however. The learning algorithms we discussed earlier require already documented information in order to be able to gain experience and learn on their own so that they can make future decisions. Neural networks, on the other hand, are capable of making decisions in the present, which makes them far more powerful and efficient. That is why neural networks are used when dealing with complex data and complicated patterns that require a system strong enough to lead to accurate results.

Recurrent Neural Networks

Now that you have a basic understanding of the simple feedforward neural networks and the concept of backpropagation, we can advance to recurrent neural networks. As you already know, the feedforward network's system works by sending data along a straight line, from node to node and layer to layer. The input is point A and the output is point B. On the other end we have the recurrent neural networks that transmit data both ways. While this is already an important change in the design of the network, it is not what makes it so special.

This type of network has the particular ability to remember all of the states a set of data goes through. After every iteration, the old state of the data will be memorized. Keep in mind that the original neural network design wasn't capable of memorization, meaning that with each iteration the previous data state would be lost. Imagine watching a video and after an ad pops up you forget what you already watched.

The structure of a recurrent neural network can be described as a series of linked nodes that consists of inputs and outputs. This system where an input becomes the output allows for highly accurate results. Now let's discuss one particular recurrent neural network that has been popularized by machine learners and data scientists in the last few years. In the next section we are going to explore the Boltzmann machine and see how to implement it in a real scenario.

The Restricted Boltzmann Machine

This neural network is a special representation of the recurrent network architecture because of the fact that it borrows certain design elements from the multilayer perceptron. For instance, the inputs and the hidden layers structures are the same as those of the perceptron, however, they are also interconnected. Take note that the structure doesn't force the network to communicate data in a particular way, namely linearly, because all elements are connected to each other to a certain degree. This means that the nodes can communicate with each other during every processing cycle, and therefore all the input variables are analyzed and modeled. Other networks only focus on the variables which can be observed. The main benefit of this system is the fact that it makes it possible for the output nodes and layer to advance.

The restricted Boltzmann machine neural network is a model that relies on an energy function. This function is what actually supports the relationship between each value and node configuration. Keep in mind that this energy value is in fact a metric which is determined mathematically and it is used to perform parameter updates. This also means that a free energy value will be present and one of your tasks will be to minimize it in order to create a powerful model.

The reason why we are discussing a restricted Boltzmann machine instead of the fundamental Boltzmann machine is because we don't want to face any scaling problems. With the simple architecture we would have a large number of nodes which would require a lot of computation power and time in order to process the data and reach a satisfactory output. This might not be a problem if we have an adequate amount of resources, however, with the increase in the number of nodes, the value of the free energy would also be higher. This value could become unmanageable, therefore, it is easier to go with a restricted model from the beginning, which implies a change in the structure, as well as the training stage. In order to restrict the network, all we need to do is apply a connectivity limit to all of the network's nodes. In other words, we need to make sure that we restrict the relation between all of the nodes that belong to a certain layer. In addition, we also need to remove the communication line between all the layers that are next to each other. These two limitations are what give this neural network its name.

Keep in mind that these restrictions aren't always the most optimal solution that will solve all of your scaling issues. Another problem we are facing is the time it takes to perform the model training. That is why we also need to implement a machine learning technique known as the Permanent Contrastive Divergence in order to lower the value of the free energy even more.

Now that the theory is out of the way, let's see this popular recurrent neural net in action in the next section and discuss the implementation of the code.

Restricted Boltzmann Machine in Practice

As mentioned, this is one of the most powerful models you can implement, especially as a beginner. You should only use this type of neural network when working with complex datasets that contain a great deal of information. To demonstrate the application of the restricted Boltzmann machine, we are going to use the MNIST handwritten digits dataset. The model will be implemented by first defining an object and its layers, vectors and various functions and attributes that are used to communicate data between the layers. Furthermore, we will apply the contrastive divergence solution in order to improve the time it takes to perform the training process.

```
class RBM(object):

def __init__(

        self,

        input=None,

        n_visible=784,

        n_hidden=500,
```

```
        w=None,

        hbias=None,

        vbias=None,

        numpy_rng=None,

        theano_rng=None

    ):
```

Let's take a break and discuss what we did so far. We have defined a new object that stands for the Boltzmann machine. As you can see there are a number of parameters attributed to this object. They define how many network nodes we have, including those that are visible and invisible, inside the hidden layer. Furthermore we have a few other attributes that are not obligatory, however, they will help in creating a better model.

```
self.n_visible = n_visible

self.n_hidden = n_hidden

if numpy_rng is None:

        numpy_rng = numpy.random.RandomState(1234)

if theano_rng is None:

        theano_rng = RandomStreams(numpy_rng.randint(2 ** 30))

if W is None:

initial_W = numpy.asarray(

        numpy_rng.uniform(

                low=-4 * numpy.sqrt(6. / (n_hidden + n_visible)),

                high=4 * numpy.sqrt(6. / (n_hidden + n_visible)),

                size=(n_visible, n_hidden)

        ),

        dtype=theano.config.floatX
```

```
)
```

The "w" attribute is used here so that we can enable the use of the GPU. In this example the GPU can handle a great deal more data processing than the CPU. It is one of the simple solutions we can use to speed up the training process. In addition we also allow data sharing between various functions that contain "theano.shared". The next step is to allow this sharing process throughout the network.

```
W = theano.shared(value=initial_W, name='W', borrow=True)

if hbias is None:

hbias = theano.shared(

        value=numpy.zeros(n_hidden,dtype=theano.config.floatX

        ),

        name='hbias',

        borrow=True

)

if vbias is None:

vbias = theano.shared(

        value=numpy.zeros(n_visible, dtype=theano.config.floatX

        ),

        name='vbias',

        borrow=True

)
```

Next, let's setup the input layer.

```
self.input = input

if not input:

self.input = T.matrix('input')
```

```python
self.W = W

self.hbias = hbias

self.vbias = vbias

self.theano_rng = theano_rng

self.params = [self.W, self.hbias, self.vbias]

def propup(self, vis):

pre_sigmoid_activation = T.dot(vis, self.W) + self.hbias

return [pre_sigmoid_activation, T.nnet.sigmoid(pre_sigmoid_ activation)]

def propdown(self, hid):

pre_sigmoid_activation = T.dot(hid, self.W.T) + self.vbias

return [pre_sigmoid_activation, T.nnet.sigmoid(pre_sigmoid_ activation)]
```

This part of the code also includes the function which communicates the activation of visible units in an upward direction towards the hidden units. This way the hidden units can determine their activation based on the samples from the visible units. This process is also performed downwards. Next, we are going to transmit the hidden layer's activations as well as the visible layer's activations.

```python
def sample_h_given_v(self, v0_sample):

pre_sigmoid_h1, h1_mean = self.propup(v0_sample)

h1_sample = self.theano_rng.binomial(size=h1_mean.shape,

n=1, p=h1_mean, dtype=theano.config.floatX)

return [pre_sigmoid_h1, h1_mean, h1_sample]

def sample_v_given_h(self, h0_sample):

pre_sigmoid_v1, v1_mean = self.propdown(h0_sample)

v1_sample = self.theano_rng.binomial(size=v1_mean.shape,

n=1, p=v1_mean, dtype=theano.config.floatX)
```

```
return [pre_sigmoid_v1, v1_mean, v1_sample]
```

We have established the connections and therefore we can handle the sampling process.

```
def gibbs_hvh(self, h0_sample):

pre_sigmoid_v1, v1_mean, v1_sample =self.sample_v_given_h(h0_sample)

pre_sigmoid_h1, h1_mean, h1_sample =self.sample_h_given_v(v1_sample)

return [pre_sigmoid_v1, v1_mean, v1_sample

        pre_sigmoid_h1, h1_mean, h1_sample]

def gibbs_vhv(self, v0_sample):

        pre_sigmoid_h1, h1_mean, h1_sample =
        self.sample_h_given_v(v0_sample)

        pre_sigmoid_v1, v1_mean, v1_sample =
        self.sample_v_given_h(h1_sample)

        return [pre_sigmoid_h1, h1_mean, h1_sample,

        pre_sigmoid_v1, v1_mean, v1_sample]
```

As you can see, the implementation of a restricted Boltzmann machine is slightly more complicated than any other models, however, it is also far more powerful. So far we have established all of our layers and neural nodes and we have finished setting up the connection lines. Furthermore, we have taken care of the sampling process. Keep in mind that sampling is used for the implementation of the permanent contrastive divergent concept, which also requires a count parameter. In this phase of the implementation, handling the free energy value is top priority. Once all of this is achieved, all we need to do is check how successful our model is.

```
def free_energy(self, v_sample):

wx_b = T.dot(v_sample, self.W) + self.hbias

vbias_term = T.dot(v_sample, self.vbias)

hidden_term = T.sum(T.log(1 + T.exp(wx_b)), axis=1)

return -hidden_term - vbias_term

def get_cost_updates(self, lr=0.1, persistent = , k=1):
```

```
pre_sigmoid_ph, ph_mean, ph_sample = self.sample_h_given_v(self.input)

chain_start = persistent

(

[

        pre_sigmoid_nvs,

        nv_means,

        nv_samples,

        pre_sigmoid_nhs,

        nh_means,

        nh_samples

        ],

        updates

) =        theano.scan(

self.gibbs_hvh,

outputs_info=[None, None, None, None, None, chain_start],

n_steps=k

)

chain_end = nv_samples[-1]

cost = T.mean(self.free_energy(self.input)) - T.mean(self.free_energy(chain_end))

gparams = T.grad(cost, self.params, consider_constant=[chain_end])

for gparam, param in zip(gparams, self.params):

updates[param] = param - gparam * T.cast(lr, dtype=theano.config.floatX)

updates = nh_samples[-1]
```

```
monitoring_cost = self.get_pseudo_likelihood_cost(updates)
```

```
return monitoring_cost, updates
```

In this section of the code we have defined the permanent contrastive divergence algorithm and we have established the learning rate parameter as well as the k parameter. As it suggests, the learning parameter refers to the speed it takes for the algorithm to learn and it gives us the option to adjust it as needed. The k parameter on the other hand represents the amount of steps which the algorithm has to perform in order to determine the value of the free energy. Now let's write the code to establish the training process.

```
def get_pseudo_likelihood_cost(self, updates):
```

```
bit_i_idx = theano.shared(value=0, name='bit_i_idx') xi = T.round(self.input)
```

```
fe_xi = self.free_energy(xi)
```

```
xi_flip = T.set_subtensor(xi[:, bit_i_idx], 1 - xi[:, bit_i_idx])
```

```
fe_xi_flip = self.free_energy(xi_flip)
```

```
cost = T.mean(self.n_visible * T.log(T.nnet.sigmoid(fe_xi_flip - fe_xi)))
```

```
        updates[bit_i_idx] = (bit_i_idx + 1) % self.n_visible
```

```
return cost
```

```
train_rbm = theano.function(
```

```
[index],
```

```
cost,
```

```
updates=updates,
```

```
givens={x: train_set_x[index * batch_size: (index + 1) *batch_size] },
```

```
name='train_rbm'
```

```
)
```

```
plotting_time = 0.
```

```
start_time = time.clock()
```

(Source: Adapted from RBM tutorial code

http://deeplearning.net/tutorial/code/deep.py retrieved in October 2019)

That's it! We have successfully implemented a restricted Boltzmann machine. This neural network might be somewhat out of your skill range as a beginner, however, it offers you a glimpse of what's to come. Furthermore, you will see that if you analyze the code line by line and read and reread the theory you will understand that a recurrent neural network such as this isn't that difficult to setup. You can even continue exploring this topic on your own, as our model can be improved and extended. The results we obtained are good, but they can always be better.

Summary

In this chapter you learned about the main types of neural networks and where they fit in the world of data science. The purpose of this section was to educate you on topics such as perceptron and recurrent neural networks. While we mostly focused on beginner-friendly theory so that you can fully understand neural networks, we have also worked with an example of the Restricted Boltzmann Machine. Keep in mind that this topic is somewhat more complex and towards the intermediary level, however, you should understand how neural networks work because they are one of the main structures used to create advanced learning and training models. Just make sure to analyze each line of code because the implementation of the Boltzmann machine can be quite lengthy when compared to basic supervised or unsupervised learning algorithms.

Chapter 8: Big Data

In data science, the purpose of supervised and unsupervised learning algorithms is to provide us with the ability to learn from complicated collections of data. The problem is that the data that is being gathered over the past few years has become massive in size. The integration of technology in every aspect of human life and the use of machine learning algorithms to learn from that data in all industries has led to an exponential increase in data gathering. These vast collections of data are known in data science as Big Data. What's the difference between regular datasets and Big Data? The learning algorithms that have been developed over the decades are often affected by the size and complexity of the data they have to process and learn from. Keep in mind that this type of data no longer measures in gigabytes, but sometimes in petabytes, which is an inconceivable number to some as we're talking about values higher than 1000 terabytes when the common household hard drive holds 1 terabyte of information, or even less.

Keep in mind that the concept of Big Data is not new. In fact, it has been theorized over the past decades as data scientists noticed an upward trend in the development of computer processing power, which is correlated with the amount of data that circulates. In the 70s and 80s when many learning algorithms and neural networks were developed, there were no massive amounts of data to process because the technology back then couldn't handle it. Even today, some of the techniques we discussed will not suffice when processing big data. That is why in this chapter we are going to discuss the growing issue of Big Data in order to understand the future challenges you will face as a data scientist.

The Challenge

Nowadays, the problem of Big Data has grown so much that it has become a specialized subfield of data science. While the previous explanation of Big Data was rudimentary with the purpose of demonstrating the problem we will face, you should know that any data is considered Big Data as long as it is a collection of information that contains a large variety of data that continues to grow at an exponential rate. This means that the data volume grows as such a speed that we can no longer keep up with it in order to process and analyze it.

The issue of Big Data appeared before the age of the Internet and online data gathering, and even if today's computers are so much more powerful than in the pre-Internet era, data is still overwhelming to analyze. Just look around you and really focus on how many aspects of your life involve technology. If you stop to think you will realize that even objects that you never considered as data recorders, save some kind of data. Now this thought might make you paranoid, however, keep in mind that most technology records information regarding its use and the user's habits in order to find better ways to improve the technology. The big problem here is that all of this technology generates too much data at a rapid pace. In addition, think about all the smart tech that's being implemented into everyone's homes in the past years. Think of Amazon's Alexa, "smart" thermostats, smart doorbells, smart everything. All of this records data and transmits it. Because of this, many professional data scientists are saying that the current volume of data is being doubled every two years. However, that's not all. The speed at which this amount of data is generated is also increasing roughly every two years. Big Data can barely be comprehended by most tech users. Just think of the difference between your Internet connection today and just five year ago. Even smartphone connections are now powerful and as easy to use as computers.

Keep in mind that we are dealing with a vicious circle when it comes to Big Data. Larger amounts of data generated at higher speeds mean that new computer hardware and software has to be developed in order to handle the data. The development of computer processing power needs to match the data generation. Essentially, we are dealing with a complex game of cat and mouse. To give you a rough idea about this issue, imagine that back in the mid-80s the entire planet's infrastructure could "only" handle around 290 petabytes of information. In the past 2 years, the world has reached a stage where it generates almost 300 petabytes in a span of 24 hours.

What all that in mind, you should understand that not all data is the same. As you probably already know, information comes in various formats. Everything generates some kind of data. Think of emails, crypto currency exchanges, the stock market, computer games, and websites. All of these create data that needs to be gathered and stored, and all of it ends up in different formats. This means that all of the information needs to be separated and categorized before being able to process it with various data science and machine learning algorithms and techniques. This is yet another Big Data challenge that we are going to continue facing for years to come. Remember that most algorithms need to work with a specific data format, therefore data exploration and analysis becomes a great deal more important and more time consuming.

Another issue is the fact that all the gathered information needs to be valued in some way. Just think of social media networks like Twitter. Imagine having to analyze all of the data ever recorded, all of the tweets that have been written since the conception of the platform. This would be extremely time consuming no matter the processing power of the computers managing it. All of the collected data would have to be pre-processed and analyzed in order to determine which data is valuable and in good condition. Furthermore, Big Data like what we just discussed raises the issue of security. Again, think about social media platforms, which are famous for data gathering. Some of the data includes personal information that belongs to the users and we all know what a disaster a Big Data breach can be. Just think of the recent Cambridge Analytica scandal. Another example is the European Union's reaction to the cybersecurity threats involving Big Data which led to the creation of the General Data Protection Regulation with the purpose of defining a set of rules regarding data gathering. Company data leaks can be damaging, but Big Data leaks lead to international disasters and changes in governments. But enough about the fear and paranoia that surrounds today's Big Data. Let's discuss the quality and accuracy of the information, which is what primarily concerns us.

A Big Data collection never contains a consistent level of quality and value when it comes to information. Massive datasets may contain accurate and valuable data that we can use, however, without a doubt it also involve a number of factors that lead to inaccuracy. One of the first questions you need to ask yourself is regarding those who have recorded the data and prepared the datasets. Have they made some assumptions in order to fill in the blanks? Have they always recorded nothing but facts and accurate data? Furthermore, you need to concern yourself with the type of storage system that was used to hold on to that data and who had access to it. Did someone do anything to change the data? Was the storage system damaged in some way that led to the corruption of a large number of files? In addition, you need to consider the way that data was measured. Imagine four devices being used in the same area to measure the temperature of the air. All of that data was recorded, but every device shows a different value. Which one of them holds the right values? Which one has inaccurate measurements? Did someone make any mistakes during the data gathering process?

Big Data poses many challenges and raises many questions. There are many variables that influence the quality and the value of data and we need to consider them before getting to the actual data. We have to deal with the limitations of technology, the possibility of human error, faulty equipment, badly written algorithms, and so on. This is why Big Data became a specialization of its own. It is highly complex and that is why we are taking this section of the book to discuss the fundamentals of Big Data and challenges you would face as a data scientist if you choose to specialize in it.

Applications in the Real World

Big Data is a component of Data Science, which means that as long as something generates and records data, this field will continue being developed. Therefore if you are still having doubts regarding your newly acquired skill, you should stop. Just think about a market crash. Imagine it as bad as any other financial disasters in the last century. This event would generate a great deal of data, personal, commercial, scientific and so on. Someone will have to process and analyze everything and that would take years no matter how many data scientists you would have available.

However, catastrophes aside, you will still have to rely on a number of pre-processing, processing and analysis in order to work with the data. The only difference is that datasets will continue to grow and in the foreseeable future we will no longer deal with small datasets like the ones we are using in this book for practice. Big Data is the future, and you will have to implement more powerful learning models and even combine them for maximum prediction accuracy. With that being said, let's explore the uses of Big Data in order to understand where you would apply your skills:

1. Maintenance: Sounds boring, but with the automation of everything, massive amounts of data are produced and with it we can determine when a certain hardware component or tool will reach its breaking point. Maintenance is part of every industry whether we're talking about manufacturing steel nails or airplanes. Big Data recorded in such industries will contain data on all the materials that were used and the various attributes that describe them. We can process this information and achieve a result that will immediately tell us when a component or tool should

expire or need maintenance. This is a simple example of how Big Data analysis and data science in general can be useful to a business.

2. Sales: Think of all the online platforms and shops that offer products or services. More and more of the turn up every single day. Large businesses are even warring with each other over the acquisition of data so that they can better predict the spending habits of their customers in order to learn how to attract those who aren't interested or how to convince the current ones to make more purchases. Market information is generated at a staggering pace and it allows us to predict certain human behavioral patterns that can generate more business and the improvement of various products and services.

3. Optimization: Big Data is difficult and costly to process and analyze, however, it is more than worth it since corporations are investing more and more into data scientists and machine learners. This kind of data analysis provides them with the much needed information to make their business more efficient and well-optimized. The larger a company is, the more cracks can be found through which they lose time and money. Predicting various costs and market trends can have a massive impact on a company's or even government's spending habits.

As you can see, analyzing Big Data is one of the next steps in data science as more and more data becomes available. Try to visualize the fact that the global society has generated nearly 90% of all information ever recorded in only two years. Every bit of data is valuable to some degree and you will have to learn all the algorithms and techniques that will help you process Big Data. With that being said, let's take a brief look at some of these techniques that are in use today to explore and process vast amounts of information.

Analyzing Big Data

In the previous chapters we have discussed a number of supervised and unsupervised learning algorithms that are used to explore, process, and analyze data. Additionally, we have also explored neural networks with the purpose of creating powerful models that can deliver accurate results. However, keep in mind that so far we talked about regular datasets. As previously mentioned, Big Data is different. Fortunately, some of the techniques and algorithms you learned can also be used to classify Big Data. In this section we will briefly summarize which methods can be used to process massive volumes of data.

When it comes to supervised learning algorithms you can use support vector machines, the Naïve Bayes algorithm, Boosting algorithm, the Maximum Entropy Method and more. Some of these are beyond a beginner's scope, therefore we did not focus on them in this book. However, you still have some options. Furthermore, you can also use a number of classification techniques such as the K-nearest neighbor algorithm or Decision Trees. Remember that classification simply involves discrete class attributes, while regression involves continuous class attributes. To solve Big Data regression problems you can use both the linear and logistic regression methods.

On the other side we have unsupervised learning algorithms which use unlabeled data in order to classify it by performing a comparison operation on all the data features. In this case you can rely on clustering algorithms, such as the K-means clustering algorithm we discussed earlier. Other techniques you can use are the Adaptive Resonance Theory and the Self Organizing Maps. Feel free to explore these last two on your own. Furthermore, you pursue clustering techniques at a deeper level because they are excellent when working with Big Data. For instance, you can use supervised clustering methods, which involve determining clusters that have a high probability density regarding the individual classes. Ideally, you want to use supervised clustering algorithms only when you have target variables and training sets which included them inside a cluster.

Another option is using unsupervised clustering techniques because they can lower the value of the intercluster similarity and therefore increase it. Keep in mind that these methods are best used on a specific function. K-means clustering is one of these techniques and it remains one of the most popular ones in use even when it comes to Big Data.

Finally, we have semi-supervised clustering algorithms. In this case we have more than just a similarity parameter. This category of clustering methods allows us to make modifications to the domain information. This way clustering can be significantly improved. This information can also act as limitations between the observations variables.

As a beginner, if you attempt working with Big Data, you should focus on using binary classifiers such as the support vector machines you learned about, or data classifiers such as decision trees. Stick to what is familiar for now, however, you should always feel encouraged to experiment on your own. As you can see there are many algorithms and techniques and we can fit only so much in one book. Feel free to use the knowledge you gained so far because it is all you need to get started on your own.

Summary

This chapter was a brief summary of what Big Data involves. You learned the history and fundamentals of this concept, as well as why you should consider focusing more on this topic. Data is generated all around us and soon, smaller datasets will be a thing of the past. Remember that information is generated at an exponential rate and currently our computers and the current number of data scientists and machine learners cannot catch up. There are even Big Data sets that have been gathered over a span of 20 years and they are still waiting to be processed and analyzed. This is a specialization of the future and you should seek to use what you have learned so far on such massive volumes of data. Some of the algorithms you studied can be applied as they are, while some need to be adapted. Use the toolkit you gathered so far and explore how it is to work with Big Data.

Conclusion

Congratulations are in order, as you successfully completed your fundamental training in data science. You came a long way from learning how to install your Python work environment. Sit back and allow time to solidify your knowledge because you have just processed a great deal of information. Data science isn't a light topic, and some of the techniques and algorithms you explored can be challenging.

Now that you have finished learning the basics, you should take the time to go over this book one more time to make sure you didn't overlook anything. It is vital that you understand the theory behind these learning algorithms and analysis techniques before you advance to the next stage. Take what you have learned so far, and make sure to practice every concept on your own with one of the widely available open source datasets. By learning everything in a structured manner and applying it into practice, you will become a data scientist in no time!

Bibliography

Albon, C. (2018). *Machine learning with Python cookbook: practical solutions from preprocessing to deep learning.* Sebastopol, CA: OReilly Media.

Garreta Raúl, & Moncecchi, G. (2013). *Learning scikit-learn: machine learning in Python: experience the benefits of machine learning techniques by applying them to real-world problems using Python and the open source scikit-learn library.* Birmingham, UK: Packt Publishing Ltd.

Géron Aurélien. (2019). *Hands-on machine learning with Scikit-Learn and TensorFlow: concepts, tools, and techniques to build intelligent systems.* Beijing ; Boston ; Farnham ; Sebastopol ; Tokyo: OReilly Media.

Zaccone, G., & Karim, M. R. (2018). *Deep Learning with TensorFlow: Explore neural networks and build intelligent systems with Python, 2nd Edition.* Birmingham: Packt Publishing.

www.ingramcontent.com/pod-product-compliance
Lightning Source LLC
Chambersburg PA
CBHW071113050326
40690CB00008B/1207